THIRD
EYE
MEDITATIONS

Introduction

What this Book Can Do for You

As a hippie flower child in the 1960s, I was desperately seeking higher awareness. I read every book I could lay hands on about what Buddhists call *nirvana* or *satori*—the state of spiritual enlightenment. We hippies were trying to get there through LSD. That didn't work out for me. I didn't come down from the drug for months and experienced perpetual, terrifying LSD flashbacks.

However, once I recovered, I lay on my bed one day (clearly clueless, I didn't even know meditation should be practiced in seated position) and prayed for a "meditation." Immediately an intense flow of energy rushed through my body from my toes to the top of my head. I was plugged into a cosmic electric socket, but in a most ecstatic way, without drugs. I figured this is "meditation." Little did I know it was not only my first meditation but also *kundalini* awakening. (Kundalini is a spiritual energy that flows up through the body and is considered difficult to attain.)

This was pure beginner's luck. I still didn't know how to meditate. But a friend introduced me to Transcendental Meditation (known commonly as "TM"), and, at age 21, off to India I went. I then experienced the uncanny blessing of 22 years living in the ashrams and six years serving on the personal staff of Maharishi Mahesh Yogi, founder of TM and guru of the Beatles.

After that, I was fortunate to study with Peter Meyer, founder of Teaching of Intuitional Metaphysics, who taught me how to tap, test, trust, and follow the voice of my higher self, and how to ask for and receive spiritual experiences and inner guidance at will.

But what if you have no Maharishi or Meyer to learn from? What if you've tried to meditate with little to no results? What if all you achieve is boredom or a headache? This can be a frustrating, hit-or-miss ordeal.

Yet meditation can be easy and enjoyable when you learn from someone who has practiced and taught it for over 50 years. I started with no spiritual skills, but I learned from masters who guided me step-by-step from point A to B and through the alphabet. These masters trained me to teach meditation from point A to traverse that same alphabet. My goal in this book is to help you succeed in meditating quickly and effortlessly so you can enjoy the benefits of a stress-free, joyous, fulfilling life.

By practicing the methods in this book, you can:

- Enjoy deep relaxation and contentment.

- Open your third eye and supersensory perception.

- Discover who you really are.

- Experience higher states of consciousness.

- Fulfill your true heart's desires and purpose.

- Improve your relationships, health, and success.

- Contribute to greater planetary balance and world peace.

Though I already have fifteen other spiritual self-help books in print, none of those books is solely devoted to the art of guided meditation. This is that book I've always wanted to write, which can bring you untold benefits.

Part I

Illuminating Your True Self

Chapter 1

Open the Doorway to Infinite Consciousness

Do you believe you don't have time to meditate? Do you think you can't meditate? Do you have no clue how to get started, or did you try to meditate but stopped doing the practice out of frustration?

Today meditation is more popular than ever. More than 14% of American adults say they practice it. Its advantages to health, well-being, creativity, longevity, and happiness are incredibly profound and have been scientifically verified.

Though millions try to meditate, many don't achieve a deep state of restful alertness and therefore don't get the relaxing, healing, spiritually uplifting effects they desire. This book can be the answer. It offers a simple, natural, enjoyable way to meditate—"guided meditation." This effortless practice can produce powerful, practical, positive results without previous talent, skill, training, or practice.

Guided meditation is a way to be led step-by-step, moment-by-moment, through the process. Just read the words, which take you into deep meditation and awaken higher aspects of your being. Or for even better results, record the words onto your phone, tablet, or computer. Then play back the recording and follow the simple instructions.

Practicing the meditations and affirmations in this book can infuse your body, mind, and spirit with love, light, and truth. You can receive divine inspiration, healing, and creative ideas. You can ask and receive clear intuition and inner guidance—at will. You can develop your spiritual self.

Because of the proliferation of meditation worldwide, there are many misconceptions about meditation and how it's practiced. So let's get started by debunking some meditation myths.

10 MEDITATION MYTHS

1. Meditation is mysterious, intangible, and impractical.

Meditation is not a mystery. It's an accessible, practical way to experience deep bodily relaxation and mental and emotional equanimity by taking your mind from the surface level into deeper and deeper levels, until your mind settles down to a state beyond all conflict and experiences inner peace and contentment.

2. Meditation is something weird and woo-woo that hippies from California do.

People from all walks of life practice meditation and get helpful, positive results. Through meditation, you can become healthier, happier, and more fulfilled. Meditation helps you solve a multitude of mundane, everyday problems.

3. Meditation is hard, bordering on impossible.

If you try to concentrate, strain, or blank your mind, you'll find meditation difficult, even unattainable. However, that's not actually meditation. The guided meditations in this book are effortless and relaxing.

4. Meditation requires tremendous skill and discipline.

If you're alive and breathing and can follow simple instructions, you can practice the easy, step-by-step guided meditations in this book.

5. No one has time to meditate in today's demanding world. It's a practice for an age when life moved much slower.

Today it's more vital than ever to take a few moments and settle down to inner peace. Otherwise the stress of modern life can overwhelm you and damage your health. You would be wise to make meditation a priority. This book offers many short meditations you can practice in three minutes or less.

6. Meditation conflicts with certain religious beliefs.

No matter what religion you follow, you can meditate. People of all major religions meditate. Meditation leads you to deep relaxation and inner peace. No religion is anti-peace or anti-relaxation.

7. People who are impatient or restless can't meditate.

Even if you think you can't sit still, you can meditate anyway. Just begin by taking three slow, deep breaths to settle down. Then just follow the instructions in the meditations in this book.

8. People can't meditate if they're too tired.

The reason you think you're too tired to meditate is because you don't meditate. If you meditated, you wouldn't feel so tired. You'd feel fresher, more alert, and more effective in everyday life.

9. Old people can't meditate.

If you think you're too old to meditate, you can't afford *not* to meditate at your age. As time ticks by, it's more vital than ever to keep your body healthy and mind alert. Meditation is scientifically proven to reverse such signs of aging as near-point vision and diminished brain functioning.

10. People can't meditate if they don't believe in God.

Meditation is not dependent on religious beliefs, because it's not necessarily a religious practice. It can be religious or spiritual, but it can also just be a way to settle the body into deep relaxation and quiet the mind into inner peace. People of all faiths and people of no faith can meditate.

SO WHAT'S "GUIDED MEDITATION"?

First I'll tell you what "guided meditation" is not: It requires no mantra. It isn't chanting OM, forcing your body into pretzel position, sitting with a stiff and rigid spine without back support, blanking your mind, or straining to concentrate.

Rather than advising you to "Sit down, close your eyes, and watch your breathing" (or similar ineffectual instructions), this book will guide you through each meditation step-by-step in great detail.

Ideally, read and record the words of each meditation onto your phone, tablet, or computer. After that, sit quietly with eyes closed and listen as you play back the meditation. Or, alternately, just read the words and follow the instructions in this book. This will lead you through the process of "guided meditation." It's that simple!

The book is written in a particular order to help you gradually deepen your meditation practice. So it's best to practice these meditations in the order they are written. However, if you'd like to choose a particular subject to explore in your meditation practice, just go to the Appendix on page 189 and find one.

WHY "THIRD EYE" MEDITATION?

Through the window of your two eyes, you view the ever-changing landscape of this magnificent world. Your five senses of seeing, hearing, tasting, smelling, and feeling are your vehicles of perception.

But there's a sixth sense. With this sixth, higher sense perception, you can open the gateway to subtler realms. Through your inner eye you can view an invisible world of multiple dimensions, spiritual planes filled with light, and alternate realities of indescribable wonders. This eye of illumination, wisdom, and intuition is aptly named "the third eye."

In India this third eye is known as *ajna chakra*—a subtle-energy plexus in the middle of your brain, seated in the pineal gland. Through this portal of higher vision, you can see beyond the narrow corridor observed by your physical eyes.

This book is named *Third Eye Meditations* because its practices lead you to higher awareness as you visualize (with your mind's eye, a.k.a. third eye) what is being described. However, to practice guided meditation successfully, your third eye doesn't need to already be open.

If you believe "I can't visualize," that won't hinder your success. You don't need any skill or talent in order to receive the expected results. You just need to follow the directions on the page, step-by-step, which will take you progressively deeper into meditation.

Visualization can be hard if you strain to focus or concentrate on making pictures in your mind's eye. But the meditations in this book are not that. They're simple instructions to follow, which guide you into meditation automatically.

These are called "third eye meditations" because they can help you open your third eye. By practicing them, you can develop clairvoyant, clairaudient, and clairsentient abilities. You can become more sensitive to subtle experiences and travel to wondrous, ecstatic destinations in inner space.

WHAT'S "AFFIRMATION"?

Another method used in this book is "affirmation." I like to call these "spoken meditations." These powerful statements, verbalized audibly, can help you expand your awareness, manifest your heart's desires, and effect positive change for yourself and the entire planet. They can remove blockages and clear a pathway for deepening your experiences.

Buddha tells us, in the first verse of the first chapter of the *Dhammapada* (the essential Buddhist scripture):

"All that we are is the result of what we have thought: it is founded on our thoughts, it is made up of our thoughts. If a person speaks or acts with an evil thought, pain follows him or her, as the wheel follows the foot of the ox that draws the carriage ... If a person

*speaks or acts with a pure thought, happiness follows him or her,
like a shadow that never leaves him."*[1]

In this verse, Buddha is saying we create our own circumstances primarily through our thoughts, but also through our speech and actions. It might be difficult to control the thousands of random thoughts streaming through your mind each day. But you can easily control your words and deeds.

For example, if you constantly say, "I am so poor, I am so out of shape, I am so unhappy, I am so sick," etc., then I guarantee these results will appear in your life. If, on the other hand, you often say, "I am wealthy, I am fit, I am happy, I am in perfect health," etc., then these results will manifest.

Master Jesus tells us, *"Not that which goeth into the mouth defileth a man; but that which cometh out of the mouth, this defileth a man."*[2] In order to become the conscious captain of your ship of destiny, be mindful of what comes out of your mouth. Consciously speak words and engage in actions that support your goals. Affirmations in this book can help you do that.

Some of the affirmations in this book declare the most idealistic outcomes for our planet, such as ecological balance and world peace. These might seem impossible goals. But nothing is impossible in Spirit. Through every thought, word, and deed, you contribute not only to your personal destiny, but also to our planetary destiny. You have much more power than you could ever imagine.

Anyone who has ever achieved greatness has done so despite all odds, despite naysayers, and despite self-sabotaging internal demons. It's just a matter of making a fixed decision to fulfill a goal and making strides through consistency of purpose and persistence in the direction of reaching that goal. It's about moving forward relentlessly, never wavering, and never giving up.

WHAT'S THE GOAL OF MEDITATION?

I think everyone has a different idea of what meditation is and what it can do. You might want to lower your blood pressure or reduce pain. But is that all there is to it? In the counterculture of the 1960s, we were seeking higher consciousness through LSD. We followed Timothy Leary and Richard Alpert (later known as Ram Dass) and read *The Psychedelic Experience* and *The Tibetan Book of the Dead*.

But drugs aren't the answer. Meditation is the best and fastest way to speed up your spiritual evolution and expand your awareness. After fifty years of meditating, I believe meditation is the panacea of all ills. It brings you back to your center, makes you relaxed and content, and heals all kinds of problems. Just by meditating, pains vanish, emotions stabilize, and happiness grows.

Above all, if you're willing to practice meditation regularly and not give up, you'll open the doorway to the ultimate goal. You'll attain freedom (a.k.a. *moksha)* from the wheel of action and its consequences (a.k.a. *karmic law),* with its perpetual rounds of birth and death, and you'll discover the truth of your being, which is infinite consciousness. You'll realize who you really are. You'll become yourself.

Let's get started on guided meditation practice in the next chapter, now!

Chapter 2

Open the Doorway to Guided Meditation

Meditation is a powerful doorway to the miraculous. It's not just about improving health or increasing mental clarity. It leads you beyond this mundane world into realms of wondrous miracles and supernal bliss. What does this mean? We human beings experience three basic states of consciousness in everyday life:

1. Waking State

Right now you're in the waking state. You're reading this book and your mind is focused on these pages. You're conscious of your thoughts and surroundings through the five senses of seeing, hearing, tasting, smelling, and feeling. Through these senses, you experience waking life.

2. Deep Sleep State

At night you experience a state of deep sleep. In that state, your mind and senses are completely at rest. You aren't thinking thoughts or experiencing anything through the senses. Your identity and personality temporarily disappear while you undergo a natural rejuvenation process.

3. Dream State

You experience REM (rapid-eye-movement) sleep at various points throughout the night while you're dreaming. Your senses and mind are actively creating various scenarios that you experience as though they were real. But when you wake, you realize they were just fantasies.

The Fourth State

Beyond waking, dreaming, and sleeping, there's a fourth state of consciousness. In India it's literally called the "fourth" *(turiya)*—a higher state of awareness also known as transcendental consciousness *(nirvana, satori,* or *samadhi).*

In that state of "restful alertness," your mind is quiet and your body is deeply relaxed. You experience profound inner peace, quietude, contentment, relaxation, integration, perfection, wholeness, oneness, and absolute bliss consciousness *(satchitananda).*

Throughout the ages, people have believed this fourth state is nearly impossible to attain, and requires tremendous discipline, effort, and renunciation. But I don't agree. You can experience this state by practicing the guided meditations in this book.

SCIENTIFIC RESEARCH ON MEDITATION

Meditation has been scientifically proven to improve many aspects of life. If you're not yet convinced meditation is right for you, here's a brief review of recent scientific research. A USA government agency known as National Center for Complementary and Integrative Health (NCCIH) reports these meditation benefits:[1]

1. Reduces back pain more effectively than just usual medical care.

2. Reduces the severity and pain of irritable bowel syndrome (IBS) symptoms.

3. Reduces stress-related ulcerative colitis flare-ups.

4. Reduces chemical identifiers of inflammation and regulates the immune system.

5. Reduces stress-induced inflammation better than other health programs.

6. Reverses psychological distress, anxiety, depression, anger/hostility, poor coping ability, and chronic insomnia, and aids restful sleep.

7. Is more effective in smoking cessation, relapse prevention, and cravings than standard behavioral smoking-cessation treatment.

8. May slow, stall, or even reverse aging-related changes in the brain.

9. Reduces negative menopausal symptoms.

10. Creates more folds in the outer layer of the brain. This is believed to increase the brain's ability to process information.

11. Lowers blood pressure, according to NCCIH and the American Heart Association.

12. Reduces stress, anxiety, pain, and depression while enhancing mood and self-esteem in lung cancer patients, according to the American College of Chest Physicians.

13. The Society for Integrative Oncology (SIO) recommends meditation to breast cancer patients to reduce stress, anxiety, depression, and fatigue, and to improve quality of life.

14. An NCCIH-funded meditation study found changes in spirituality were associated with better mental health and quality of life.

PREPARING TO MEDITATE

Before you practice the first guided meditation in this book, let's get ready first. The best way to start is to record the meditation on your device. Then, before playing it back, prepare for meditation in a few short steps. Here's how:

1. Make a recording of the meditation.

It's possible to practice the guided meditations in this book just by reading them. But ideally, it's better to record the words onto your phone, tablet, or computer and then play back the recording and listen with your eyes closed.

Here are instructions for recording the meditations:

Go to page 20, line 4, to record the first meditation, titled the "Clearing Meditation." Record the meditation in a soft, slow, gentle, soothing voice. You'd be surprised at how soothing your voice can be just by slowing the tempo and turning down the volume.

Please pause for a few seconds whenever you see ellipses (. . .) in the text. Those indicate a brief pause during the meditation. If the instructions say to repeat affirmations audibly, please pause at the ellipses and leave yourself enough silent time to repeat those affirmations verbally when you play back the meditation.

If you see instructions in brackets [ ] that tell you to record a certain number of seconds or minutes of silence, just continue recording in silence for that length of time.

2. Take a lavatory break.

Go to the lavatory before practicing any of the longer meditations in this book. It's okay to take bathroom breaks during meditation, but, if possible, it's better not to interrupt meditation. If you need a bathroom break anytime during meditation, please pause the playback, go quickly, and then return to meditation. "Holding it in" is not conducive to deep meditation.

3. Find a comfortable, quiet place to sit.

Turn off the TV and all phones within earshot. Place pets in a separate area. Tell kids you want quiet time and they shouldn't disturb you. Put a "Do Not Disturb" sign on your door if you think someone will interrupt you.

Sit in a comfortable chair. Or sit on your bed and prop up pillows as back support. Or sit on the floor with your back supported by pillows against a wall. Comfort is the most vital feature of deep, relaxing meditations, so please sit with back support. For most people, sitting on the floor without back support is not conducive to relaxation and therefore not helpful for deep meditation. Please don't lie down while meditating. It's better to be seated, because lying down might lull you to sleep.

4. Drink some water.

Drink some pure, fresh water at room temperature (not soda, not coffee, not tea) until you feel fully hydrated. Keep a glass or bottle of water nearby. Yes, it's okay to drink water during meditation whenever you want. It's also okay to have bad posture, shift your weight, scratch, burp, fart, and engage in any other natural processes. Sitting stiff as an unmoving board while feeling itchy or in pain is not conducive to a relaxing meditation.

5. Start the playback, close your eyes, and follow the instructions.

Start the playback of the meditation at a soft volume. Close your eyes and listen. Follow the instructions of your own voice guiding you into meditation.

If you're not able to make a recording, simply read the words from this book. You can experience successful meditation this way. But, if possible, I recommend recording and playing back the meditation.

During many of the meditations in this book, you'll be guided to take several deep breaths. One note is important about deep breaths: Each time you're asked to take a deep breath, that means just take one big deep breath—not several and not hyperventilating. When you're asked to breathe normally, just relax and breathe quietly. Don't continue taking deep breaths throughout the meditation. Just follow the instructions.

• • •

Here's the first meditation for you to record and play back:

CLEARING MEDITATION

Please record the following meditation on your device:

If you are listening to this as a recording, please close your eyes now and keep them closed throughout the meditation, until I tell you to open them.

Peace, peace, be still. Be still and be at peace. Peace, peace, be at peace. Be still and be at peace. Take a deep breath of divine love. Breathe in . . . and out . . . Take a deep breath of divine light. Breathe in . . . and out . . . Take a deep breath of relaxation. Breathe in . . . and out . . . Take a big deep breath to go deeper. Breathe in . . . and out . . . Now relax and breathe normally. Deeper, deeper, deeper into the wells of Spirit, into the silence of being. Peace, peace, be still. Be still and be at peace.

We now recognize there is one power and one presence in the universe and in our lives—the divine presence. We are one with the power, the light, love, peace, joy, and purity of this presence now. We are one with the truth of our being, with the light of Spirit. One with wholeness, oneness, and pure consciousness.

We therefore claim a perfect, profound, clearing meditation now that proceeds perfectly with divine order and timing. We know that during this meditation you receive spiritual healing, deep relaxation and serenity, as much as you can comfortably enjoy. You receive perfect peace, wholeness, and oneness. You receive clearing, cleansing, and lifting of your energy field. Your energy field is filled with divine love and light. You now receive all that is wise for you to receive in this meditation, all that I have spoken or better. Thank you Spirit, and SO IT IS.

Please repeat audibly some affirmations after me now:

I AM in control . . . I AM the only authority in my life . . . I AM divinely protected by the light of my being . . . I close off my aura and body of light . . . to the lower levels of mind . . . and I open to the spiritual world . . .

I invoke the divine presence . . . to eliminate any and all negations and limitations . . . that have lowered the vibration of my energy field . . . I now dispel all negations . . . of worry, doubt, fear . . . confusion, limitation, unworthiness . . . anger, guilt, blame . . . sadness and pain . . . and any other thoughts and emotions . . . that no longer serve me . . . and that do not reflect the truth of my being . . . I now welcome and accept thoughts . . . of inner peace, love, certainty . . . strength, courage, happiness . . . contentment, trust, faith . . . joy, ease, and comfort . . . I AM in control . . . I thank Spirit, and SO IT IS . . .

I now heal any interfering beings . . . from the astral plane . . . that might be blocking . . . this process of meditation now . . . Beloved ones, you are unified . . . with the truth of your being . . . You are lifted in divine love . . . You are forgiven of all guilt and shame . . . You are healed, loosed, and released . . . from loss, pain, confusion, and fear . . . Divine love and divine light . . . fill and surround you now . . . Attachment to the earth . . . no longer binds you . . . You are free to go . . . into the divine light now, dear ones . . . Go now in peace and love.

I now call upon Spirit . . . to cut any and all psychic ties . . . cords, connections, and karmic bonds . . . between myself and any person, place, thing . . . organization, situation, circumstance . . . memory, experience, or addiction . . . that is unduly influencing me . . . or has interfered in my life . . . or has control over me now . . . These psychic bonds are now lovingly . . . cut, cut, cut, cut, cut, cut, cut, cut . . . lifted, loved, healed, released . . . dissolved and completely let go . . . into the light of divine love and truth . . . Thank you, Spirit, and SO IT IS.

Now take another big deep breath. Breathe in . . . and out . . . Then breathe normally. Peace, peace, be still. Be still and be at peace. Perfect peace, perfect peace, perfect peace. Be still and be at peace . . .

Now relax your mind and go deeper. Turn within, away from the outer world and into the inner world. Let go of the environment. Release, loose, and let go of all cares and concerns of the day. Any and all limiting thoughts or negative beliefs you have brought into this meditation, now give them over to Spirit. Release and let go of them now as you take another big deep breath. Breathe in . . . and out . . . Then breathe normally and easily.

Now become aware of your physical body . . . Anywhere you feel any sensation, tension, or stress, just allow your attention and awareness to simply rest on that place or places within the body that need healing. As you place attention on those sensations, take a few moments of quietude to allow them to dissipate . . . [Record fifteen seconds of silence here.] Now take a deep breath to go deeper, deeper, into the wells of Spirit . . .

Now become aware that your physical body is becoming very relaxed, quiet, and still. As your breathing becomes less, your heart rate settles down. Every part of your body is deeply relaxed. Take a big deep breath to relax your whole body. Breathe in . . . and out . . . Then breathe normally. Take another big deep breath to fill up your entire body with peace. Breathe in . . . and out . . . Then breathe easily and normally.

Perfect peace, perfect peace, perfect peace . . . Be still and be at peace . . . Completely let go and relax . . . Now take a big deep breath to go deeper. Breathe in . . . and out . . . Then breathe normally. Deeper,

deeper, deeper into the wells of Spirit, into the silence of being. Relax, let go, and be at peace . . .

Now notice that as your body is deeply relaxed, your mind is also at peace. Your mind is still, silent, and at peace, like a still, freshwater pond without a ripple. Your mind is serene, tranquil, and at peace. Now take a few more moments to enjoy deep relaxation and inner peace in silence and quietude . . . . [Record two minutes of silence here.]

Peace, peace be still. Be still and be at peace. Peace, peace, be still. Be still and be at peace . . . Perfect peace, perfect peace. Be still and be at peace.

With gratitude in your heart, you will now be coming forth from this meditation. First lean forward very slightly in your chair. Then take a big deep breath, and as you exhale, pretend you're quickly, vigorously, blowing out a candle. This kind of breath brings you out of meditation quickly.

Take a deep breath like this right now, and pretend you're blowing out a candle . . . Then take a second deep breath and blow out another candle . . . Become aware that your mind is one with Spirit, one with the truth of being. Your conscious mind is now united with divine mind.

Take another big deep breath and blow out another candle . . . Now become aware of your physical body . . . Your physical body has been transformed and lifted. It is one with the divine body and is transmuted into a radiant body of pure light, brilliance, splendor, and magnificence, in robust health and well-being.

Now take another big deep breath and blow out a candle as you become aware of the environment, yet still keeping your eyes closed . . . Become aware of your body sitting in the chair, the space around you, coming back to this time and place. Know that you bring into the environment all the peace, love, and joy you have gained from this meditation. As you move into daily life, you now vibrate and radiate love all around you in every precious moment. You are a brilliant being of light. You are a walking, talking, breathing, living vessel of Spirit, and you realize the magnificence of your being.

Now take four deep vigorous breaths and blow out four candles. Then come all the way back to objective and subjective balance and open your eyes . . .

Now repeat the following affirmation audibly with your eyes open:

I AM alert . . . I AM awake . . . I AM very alert . . . I AM very awake . . . I AM objectively and subjectively balanced . . . I AM in control . . . I AM the only authority in my life . . . I AM divinely protected by the light of my being . . . Thank you, Spirit, and SO IT IS.

After you come out of each meditation in this book, please take a few moments to describe your experiences by writing in a notebook, a journal, or a computer file. Then later you can return and revisit what you've experienced and learned from each meditation.

Now that you've experienced clearing and well-being through this first meditation, in the next chapter, you'll practice meditations that help you increase divine love and light in your energy field.

Chapter 3

Open the Doorway to Divine Love and Light

Meditation can lift you out of everyday mundane existence and bring you to heavenly realms of awareness. Though you may not yet know that you're a divine being, filled with love, light, and energy, you can begin to experience that through meditation. In this chapter you'll open your heart, mind, and soul to Spirit. You'll lift your vibration to higher consciousness and begin to identify yourself as your true nature, which is perfect and whole in every way.

If possible, record the meditations in this book onto your phone, tablet, or computer, and then play back the recordings to enjoy these deep meditative experiences.

SPIRITUAL LIFTING INVOCATION

Please record the following invocation on your device:

If you are listening to this invocation as a recording, please close your eyes now and keep them closed until I tell you to open them.

Take a big deep breath of divine love. Breathe in . . . and out . . . Take a big deep breath of relaxation. Breathe in . . . and out . . . Take a big deep breath of inner peace. Breathe in . . . and out . . . Now breathe normally . . . Peace, peace, be still. Be still, and be at peace. Perfect peace, perfect peace, perfect peace. Be still and be at peace.

We now call upon the divine beings of light to lift your energy out of this earthly realm of duality and into the heavenly world of oneness. We call upon divine light beings, ascended masters, angels, and archangels who come in the name of God to lift your vibration to the highest octave of energy that you can comfortably enjoy now and to bless you with their loving presence.

We call upon the Holy Spirit, the Spirit of truth and wholeness, to flood your mind and body with the pure white light of truth, which fills and surrounds you now. The Holy Spirit now pervades you with the white fire of divine peace, love, and harmony. You are immersed in divine energy, love, light, and grace.

We now call upon Master Jesus to build a beauteous golden sphere of protective love and light around your energy field. We ask this brilliant, dazzling, golden light to pervade, permeate, and surround you, bringing peace, comfort, security, and energy. This radiating golden light fills you with divine love, healing, comfort, and brilliance.

We now call upon Archangel Michael to stand above, below, and on every side of this resplendent golden sphere, shining his blue flame sword of truth, bringing divine will, protection, security, and safety. The blue light of Archangel Michael surrounds, encompasses, safeguards, and shelters you now.

We now call upon Saint Germaine to fill and surround you with the violet consuming flame of transmutation. This violet fire now swirls throughout your energy field like a tornado of purifying divine light: cleansing, healing, and lifting, cleansing, healing, and lifting, cleansing, healing, and lifting every atom of your body and every inch of your energy field.

We now call forth beautiful Mother Mary and Kwan Yin to fill you with the pink light of divine love and compassion, bringing you peace, harmony, strength, and wisdom. Your heart is now filled and surrounded with pure unconditional love.

We ask the great sage Mahamuni Babaji to bless you with the clear light of enlightenment and illumination, to bring forth the energy of the Himalayan yogis, and to bathe you in the radiant light of the immortal *siddhas*—the perfected beings of India.

We now call upon the divine angels and archangels to encircle you and feed you divine energy, peace, love, and wisdom. We ask all the beings of light who are in your stream of identity to lift your vibration to universal consciousness or better.

You are the temple of living Spirit, immersed in the supernal light of divine love and peace. You are filled with the brilliance of divine light. You are at peace.

Now take a few moments of silence to bask in the glow of the ascended beings of light . . . [Record fifteen seconds of silence here.]

Now, with gratitude in your heart, keep your eyes closed as you come forth from the visualization and pretend you are blowing out four candles . . . [Record 15 seconds of silence here.] Then come all the way back to objective and subjective balance and open your eyes . . .

Now repeat the following affirmation audibly with your eyes open: *I AM alert . . . I AM awake . . . I AM very alert . . . I AM very awake . . . I AM objectively and subjectively balanced . . . I AM in control . . . I AM the only authority in my life . . . I AM divinely protected by the light of my being . . . Thank you, Spirit, and SO IT IS.*

DIVINE LOVE IMMERSION

Please record the following meditation on your device:

If you are listening to this as a recording, please close your eyes now and keep them closed throughout the meditation, until I tell you to open them.

Take a big deep breath of divine love. Breathe in . . . and out . . . Take a big deep breath of relaxation. Breathe in . . . and out . . . Take a big deep breath of inner peace. Breathe in . . . and out . . . Now breathe normally . . . Peace, peace, be still. Be still, and be at peace. Perfect peace, perfect peace, perfect peace. Be still and be at peace.

We now call upon Spirit to bring forth divine love into your being. Allow your heart to open and receive the energy and blessings of divine love. Take a big deep breath of divine love. Breathe in . . . and out . . . Now breathe normally . . . The holy presence beckons and draws you near. As you reach out to Spirit, you are held tenderly in the arms of divine love. You are lovingly caressed by the warmth of divine love, which brings comfort, solace, and peace. You deserve to be loved, and you are deeply loved by Spirit.

Breathe in . . . and out . . . Let go, let go, let go, let go. Let go, let go, let God. Now breathe normally. Divine love now fills your heart with comfort, joy, happiness, and fulfillment. The embrace of divine love pervades, permeates, and surrounds every particle of your being and heals all traces of rejection, guilt, shame, and self-loathing. Spirit is with you always, and you are never alone.

Take another big deep breath of divine love. Breathe in . . . and out . . . Let go, let go, let go, let go. Let go, let go, let God. Now breathe normally. Breathe in . . . and out . . . Deeper, deeper, deeper, into the wells of Spirit, into the silence of being. Relax, release, and be at peace.

Now breathe normally . . . Immerse yourself in the pristine, healing waterfall of pure love, and know that you are now made new in the sight of Spirit. The fountainhead of divine love pours over you and washes all self-hatred from your being. Pure love now washes away every tinge of sadness, pain, and suffering. Your heart is cleansed in the healing waters of divine love, which eliminates all false beliefs and brings you wisdom. You are now filled with self-acceptance, self-compassion, self-forgiveness, self-worth, and self-love.

Take another big deep breath of divine love. Breathe in . . . and out . . . Now breathe normally. No matter what you do, Spirit loves you. No matter what shame you feel, Spirit loves you. No matter how degraded you feel, Spirit loves you. No matter how worthless you feel, Spirit loves you. No matter what regrets you have, Spirit loves you. No matter how much you condemn yourself, Spirit still loves you.

Nothing is more powerful than divine love. It heals all and makes all things new. The medicine of divine love now transforms all false beliefs you have about yourself. You are renewed by the curative power of pure love. The collyrium of divine love now opens your eyes to reality. You see the truth, and you are set free.

The floodgates of divine love now open. Plunge into the ocean of divine love and immerse yourself in waves of bliss. You are engulfed in pure love, cleansed and purified in the holy waters. You are inundated and saturated by the tender, compassionate, loving presence of Spirit. Magnificent streams of heavenly energy vibrate and radiate within and around you. Waves of unconditional love now swell throughout your being. Bathe in the splendor of the sacred presence of Spirit, the eternal oneness of being. Lose yourself and find your true self in the waters of divine love.

See yourself through the eyes of pure love, and know that you are made whole. See and know the truth now. You are a magnificent beauteous being, conceived and born in pure love. You are divine and you are worthy. You are loved, you are radiant, and you are the embodiment of joy. Let divine love be your guide and your password to glory. Love is the only power and the only presence, and it is within you. It is you.

Now take a few moments to dwell in divine love in silence . . . [Record thirty seconds of silence here.]

Peace, peace, be still. Be still and be at peace. Perfect peace, perfect peace, perfect peace. Be still and be at peace. Now, with gratitude in your heart, keep your eyes closed as you come forth from the meditation and pretend you are blowing out four candles . . . [Record fifteen seconds of silence here.] Then come all the way back to objective and subjective balance and open your eyes . . .

Now repeat the following affirmation audibly with your eyes open:

I AM alert . . . I AM awake . . . I AM very alert . . . I AM very awake . . . I AM objectively and subjectively balanced . . . I AM in control . . . I AM the only authority in my life . . . I AM divinely protected by the light of my being . . . Thank you, Spirit, and SO IT IS.

DIVINE LIGHT RADIANCE

Please record the following meditation on your device:

If you are listening to this as a recording, please close your eyes now and keep them closed throughout the meditation, until I tell you to open them.

Take a big deep breath of divine light. Breathe in . . . and out . . . Take a big deep breath of divine love. Breathe in . . . and out . . . Take a big deep breath of relaxation. Breathe in . . . and out . . . Now breathe normally . . . Peace, peace, be still. Be still, and be at peace. Perfect peace, perfect peace, perfect peace. Be still and be at peace.

We now call upon Spirit to bring forth pure divine light into your being. Allow divine light to stream from the altar of the most high to flood your being with radiance. Divine light now fills your energy field with brilliance and glory. Take a big deep breath of divine light. Breathe in . . . and out . . . Let go, let go, let go, let go. Let go, let go, let God. Now breathe normally.

You are now surrounded and suffused with pure light—the light of Spirit. Your mind is illuminated with truth, your heart is ignited with joy, and your being is irradiated with oneness. You are the embodiment of pure divine light, right here and now. Take another big deep breath of divine light. Breathe in . . . and out . . . Deeper, deeper, deeper, into the wells of Spirit, into the silence of being. Now breathe normally.

You are now brimming with pure light. Every part and particle of your energy field is immersed in divine light. Every atom of your being is saturated with divine light. There is no darkness found anywhere within or around you. You are made of pure light, and nothing but light permeates you now.

The light of Spirit surrounds you. The presence of light moves through your being, igniting all dark corners and shining the light of truth upon all that must be revealed. The light of Spirit knows the truth and discloses divine wisdom now.

Allow divine light to reveal what has been hidden, and know the truth, which sets you free. Let the streams of pure light cascade into your being and fill you with peace. You are a divine being, worthy to experience divine light. Receive the rays of spiritual light that now beam into your being.

See the light streams rushing into your energy field as you are blessed and glorified in the light of Spirit. Lift your face towards Spirit and feel the blast of divine light washing over you, purifying you with its effulgence. See and feel the splendor of Spirit as it overtakes your being and ignites you with joy.

The light of Spirit shines brightly in your mind, emotions, body, spirit, and being. It gleams with radiance and illuminates all in its pathway. As you see and embody the magnificence of divine light, you are filled with power, tenacity, perseverance, and relentless optimism. Nothing and no one stands in your way to achieving your true heart's desires, for you are lit with the fire of spiritual strength and the passion of divine purpose.

The light of Spirit motivates and moves you in the direction of your highest good, and you are on fire, making the most of every day in powerful, positive ways. The light of Spirit illumines your pathway and shows you what direction to follow. It is the light-house of your life, and it shows you the way home—the way to your true self.

Once you find your way home, you stand in the resplendence of divine light—radiant, brilliant, and free. You are a beacon to all who seek the light. You are a way-shower to those in quest of truth. You stand in the sunshine of divine love, blazing brightly and guiding others to the straight path that leads to glory. You are loved and beloved of Spirit. Be at peace.

Now take a few moments of silence to bathe in divine light . . . [Record fifteen seconds of silence here.]

Now, with gratitude and thanksgiving for this experience, keep your eyes closed as you come forth from the meditation and pretend you are blowing out four candles . . . [Record fifteen seconds of silence here.] Then come all the way back to objective and subjective balance and open your eyes . . .

Now repeat the following affirmation audibly with your eyes open:

I AM alert . . . I AM awake . . . I AM very alert . . . I AM very awake . . . I AM objectively and subjectively balanced . . . I AM in control . . . I AM the only authority in my life . . . I AM divinely protected by the light of my being . . . Thank you, Spirit, and SO IT IS.

Please take a few moments now to write about your experiences of calling upon divine beings of light and filling your energy field with divine love and light through the powerful, lifting meditations you practiced in this chapter. In the next chapter, you'll enjoy some meditations of forgiveness and gratitude.

Chapter 4

Open the Doorway to Forgiveness and Gratitude

Forgiveness allows you to let go of the past and live in the present. Forgiving yourself is foremost. By forgiving yourself, you no longer hold resentment towards others. As you release self-inflicted guilt and shame, you throw away the scorecard of seeming wrongs you imagine others have inflicted on you. Life is too short for keeping tallies. Letting go brings peace of mind.

Though true forgiveness doesn't necessarily come easily or quickly, it's worth the effort and time invested. Research has found practicing forgiveness decreases stress, hypertension, cortisol rate, heart rate, and blood pressure, and improves health, happiness, self-esteem, mood, and psychological well-being.

Gratitude for the innumerable blessings you receive is an avenue towards inner peace. You might take these blessings for granted, but if you were to count them, you might be surprised at how rich your life is. If you live in gratitude, you become wealthy in Spirit. No longer do you dwell in lack. Instead you dwell in abundance. And that internal abundance materializes as material prosperity.

Research links gratitude with decreased stress, depression, substance abuse, and suicidal thoughts, and improvements in academic performance, well-being, sleep, self-esteem, happiness, trust in people, and resilience recovering from PTSD.

Whenever you use affirmations, say them audibly with confidence in a strong, clear, assertive voice. One added tip is that affirmations are more powerful when you pretend your higher self is saying the affirmations through you. In other words, imagine it isn't your ego speaking the affirmations. It's your higher self.

SELF-FORGIVENESS HEALING AFFIRMATION

The best way to forgive others is to first forgive yourself. This affirmation can help you do this. Speak it audibly in a convincing, confident voice:

> *I call upon the Holy Spirit to release all guilt and shame that*
> *I have held in my heart. I recognize that I have acted in ways*
> *that have been unfeeling, cruel, spiteful, pitiless, and seemingly*
> *unforgivable. But I no longer need to hold on to self-condemnation*
> *and self-deprecation. I no longer need to judge myself harshly.*

I admit that I have committed many wrongdoings, whether thoughtless and in haste, or whether premeditated and calculated. I know my higher self would never hurt anyone or do any harm. My actions have been ignorant and oblivious, due to negative habits, false conditioning, unconsciousness, and seemingly involuntary, unwitting, knee-jerk reactions.

Despite my previous seeming wrongdoings, I know I always did the very best I could do in every situation, given my level of consciousness and state of mind at that time, and given the situations and circumstances I encountered. Therefore, there is no need for guilt or shame. There is no need to condemn myself for seeming errors or to hold on to the past.

I no longer create situations that inflict self-punishment. I no longer feel the need to subconsciously invent ways to hurt, harm, or sabotage myself in order to pay for seeming past crimes. I no longer sentence myself to metaphorical prison terms, chains, hard labor, solitary confinement, or other negative conditions of my own making. I no longer feel the need to suffer for past transgressions by attracting into my life abusive, self-punishing situations, such as failure, loss, pain, illness, or misery.

I now forgive myself for lack of understanding. I now forgive myself for impatience. I now forgive myself for errors. I now forgive

myself for causing pain and suffering to myself and to others. I now
forgive myself for acting in seemingly unforgivable ways. I know
that Spirit does not condemn me, so I no longer condemn myself.
And I now forgive myself for condemning myself.

I now let go of regret by placing all my seeming wrongdoings into
a big gunnysack and handing it over to Spirit. I now give over
all my abusive behavior to Spirit, knowing that I intend to do no
further harm, and I AM fully forgiven. I let go and let Spirit bring
forgiveness and blessedness into my life. I know that by divine grace
I AM healed, forgiven, lifted, and cleansed. I now let go of the need to
wallow in sorrow, remorse, and regret, and I forgive myself.

I AM a divine being of light, living in the heart of divine love.
I love myself completely, and I forgive myself completely. I
AM a child of God. I AM healed. I AM whole. I AM perfection
everywhere now. I AM perfection here now. I AM perfect exactly
as I AM, because I was created in the likeness and image of That
which is perfection. I AM loved and beloved of Spirit. SO BE IT.

Please note: In the case of substance abuse and other addictions, it's
not enough to pray for forgiveness. It's also necessary to reach out for
help and follow a treatment program diligently.

FORGIVENESS CHANT

Holding on to resentment doesn't punish the person who wronged you. It punishes you. Forgiveness isn't about condoning the other person's behavior. It's about letting go of resentment. No matter how seemingly unforgivable is the person's transgression, it's possible to let go of negative emotions that are poisoning you. Such negative emotions can cause mental or physical illness, so let them go now.

If you feel someone has wronged you, say this affirmation audibly in a commanding voice, daily, until you no longer feel charged emotions towards the person.

Spirit within me is my forgiving and releasing power.

Spirit within   (name of person)   is his/her forgiving and releasing power.

Spirit within me is my forgiving and releasing power.

Spirit within   (name of person)   is his/her forgiving and releasing power.

Spirit within me is my forgiving and releasing power.

Spirit within   (name of person)   is his/her forgiving and releasing power.

Spirit within me is my forgiving and releasing power.

Spirit within ___(name of person)___ is his/her forgiving and releasing power.

Spirit within me is my forgiving and releasing power.

Spirit within___(name of person)___ is his/her forgiving and releasing power.

I now call upon Spirit to eliminate all psychic ties and karmic bondage between ___(name of person)___ and me. These psychic ties are now lovingly and completely cut, cut, cut, cut, cut, cut, cut, cut, cut, cut, cut, cut, cut, cut, cut, lifted, loved, blessed, healed, released, dissolved, and completely let go.

I AM in control. I AM the only authority in my life. I AM divinely protected by the light of my being. My aura and body of light are now closed off to ___(name of person)___ and to all but my own inner divinity.

I AM now completely free of bondage from ___(name of person)___. I AM now forgiven and ___(name of person)___ is now forgiven. All things are cleared up between us now and forevermore, from the point of origin to the present, and from this place into the entire universe and into all dimensions. Thank you, Spirit, and SO IT IS.

GRATITUDE MEDITATION

Record the following meditation on your device:

If you are listening to this guided meditation as a recording, please close your eyes now and keep them closed until I tell you to open them.

Peace, peace, be still. Be still and be at peace. Peace, peace, be at peace. Be still and be at peace. Take a deep breath of divine love. Breathe in . . . and out . . . Take a deep breath of divine light. Breathe in . . . and out . . . Take a deep breath of gratitude. Breathe in . . . and out . . . Take a big deep breath to go deeper. Breathe in . . . and out . . . Now relax and breathe normally.

Let go, let go, let go. Let go, let go, let God. Allow your heart to open to Spirit. Imagine yourself in a beautiful bubble of light. You are filled, surrounded, and encompassed by pure light of whatever color you see in your mind's eye. That is the light of divine gratitude. Allow your heart to open to that light. Your heart is now filled with the light of perfect gratitude.

Take a few moments of silence now to think about the people and things in your life that bring you so much love and happiness . . . [Record one minute of silence here.] Now repeat after me in a strong, confident, audible voice, "Thank you, Spirit, for all these blessings" . . .

Now take a few moments of silence to contemplate the most memorable challenges and hurdles you have overcome in your life and triumphed . . . [Record one minute of silence here.] Now repeat after me in a strong, confident, audible voice, "Thank you, Spirit, for all these blessings" . . .

Now take a few moments of silence to think of people who have been enemies or who seemed to cause you pain and suffering, yet have been some of your greatest teachers . . . [Record one minute of silence here.] Now repeat after me in a strong, confident, audible voice, "Thank you, Spirit, for all these blessings" . . .

Now take a few more moments of silence to remember some of the happiest experiences you've had throughout your life . . . [Record one minute of silence here.] Now repeat after me in a strong, confident, audible voice, "Thank you, Spirit, for all these blessings" . . .

Release from your mind now any thought, feeling, or emotion of lack, deficiency, and neediness. Such thoughts are released and let go from your mind, and they are gone. You are now filled with thoughts of fullness, completeness, repletion, abundance, and plenty. The bounty of divine gifts fills you with total contentment. You are now abundantly provided for.

There is no hankering after things you don't have, for you already have everything. There is only wholeness and oneness, where lack does not exist and nothing is missing. You cannot lose anything when you already have everything. All that you are is full and nothing more can be added. You are filled and replete with fulfillment.

Now take a few moments of silence to enjoy the experience of contentment, fullness, and thanksgiving . . . [Record fifteen seconds of silence here.]

Then, with gratitude in your heart, keep your eyes closed as you come forth from the meditation and pretend you are blowing out four candles . . . [Record fifteen seconds of silence here.] Then, come all the way back to objective and subjective balance and open your eyes . . .

Now repeat the following affirmation audibly with your eyes open:

I AM alert . . . I AM awake . . . I AM very alert . . . I AM very awake . . . I AM objectively and subjectively balanced . . . I AM in control . . . I AM the only authority in my life . . . I AM divinely protected by the light of my being . . . Thank you, Spirit, and SO IT IS.

FORGIVENESS AND GRATITUDE MANTRA

Dr. Ihaleakala Hew Len cured an entire ward of court-ordered psychiatric patients in the Hawaii State Hospital. The method he used was

Ho'oponopono, created in 1976 by a female Hawaiian healer, Morrnah Simeona. Dr. Len claims he never met any of his patients. Instead, he sat at his desk, reviewed each patient's file, discovered how he was himself responsible for that patient's illness, and then cleansed himself through gratitude and forgiveness. As he cleansed himself, his patients got well.

In this process of healing, Dr. Len recognized he was the sole creator of his reality, there was no reality other than what was in his mind, there was no separation between himself and his patients, he was equally responsible for them as for himself, and therefore, if he healed himself, he would heal them.

The four easy but incredibly powerful steps in Ho'oponopono are repentance, forgiveness, gratitude, and love. You can use this method to cleanse, heal, and transform any problem in your life, another's life, or the planet's life. The mantra to use is below. You can verbalize it audibly or think it in your mind.

I am sorry.
Please forgive me.
Thank you.
I love you.

Amazingly, as you practice the mantra, it's not necessary to know exactly whom or what you're healing. It can be you, another person, or Spirit. By feeling the emotions invoked by the mantra's words, a mysterious power is activated, which heals you and your world.

Now that you've experienced forgiveness and gratitude, please take a moment to record your impressions and experiences in your journal. In the next chapter, let's open the doorway to inner strength.

Chapter 5

Open the Doorway to Inner Strength

You can enjoy a spiritually lived, mindfully managed, inner-directed, disciplined life, characterized by self-confidence, self-authority, resiliency, and fortitude within. Your inner pillar of strength is a compass that guides you in the right direction towards your divine destiny.

Without inner power, you might drift like a leaf in the wind without direction—at the mercy of others. Those who don't have your best interests at heart might unduly influence you. "Energy vampires" can get their hooks into you and control you. Toxic relationships can drain you.

"Energy sponges" are sensitive, empathic people who absorb negative energies and lower vibrations as a sponge absorbs water. People they encounter are like energy vampires, sucking them dry. By the end of the day, all they can do is collapse of drain and exhaustion.

If this sounds familiar, this chapter can drive a stake through the heart of energy vampirism, bring you freedom, and give you a powerful energy-infusion boost.

SELF-EMPOWERMENT AFFIRMATION

Speak this affirmation audibly with strength and confidence, as though your higher self is saying it through you. In other words, rather than speaking from the level of ego mind, speak with absolute conviction from your heart—your true self.

I AM in control of my life and my mind now and always.
No one and nothing has control over me.
I AM one with Spirit.
I AM merged with Spirit in complete unity and oneness.
There is one and only one.
I AM that oneness. I AM that wholeness.
I AM divinely protected by the light of my being.
I AM safe, secure, and stable.
Nothing and no one can affect me adversely.
I AM no longer subject to negative energies around me.
I close off my energy field to all lower vibrations.
And I open only to the spiritual world.
I AM free.
Thank you, Spirit, and SO IT IS.

SELF-AUTHORITY AFFIRMATION

Here's another powerful affirmation to help you overcome energy drain and vampirism and help you become self-empowered. Speak this affirmation in a strong and confident voice, with conviction.

> *I AM in control. I AM one with Spirit.*
> *I AM divinely protected by the light of my being.*
> *I close off my aura and body of light*
> *To the lower astral levels of mind,*
> *And I open to the spiritual world.*
> *Thank you, Spirit, and SO IT IS.*

ASTRAL ENTITY HEALING AFFIRMATION

Whenever you feel drained by untoward energies or vampirism, during meditation or other times, use this affirmation to heal those energies. The "dear ones" you are addressing here are energy vampires, earthbound spirits, or other negative beings that need healing. (For more information on this topic, please read my book *The Power of Auras*.)

> *Dear ones, you are healed and forgiven. You are lifted in divine*
> *love. You are bless-ed, forgiven, and released into the love, light,*
> *and wholeness of the universal Spirit. You are bless-ed, forgiven,*
> *and released into the love, light, and wholeness of the universal*

Spirit. You are bless-ed, forgiven, and released into the love, light, and wholeness of the universal Spirit. You are lifted into the light of Spirit. You are lifted into the light of Spirit. You are lifted into the light of Spirit. Divine love and light fill and surround you now. Fear and pain no longer bind you. You are free from vibrations of the physical plane. You are free to go to your perfect place of expression, dear ones. You are lifted into divine light now. Go into the light now in peace and in love.

PILLAR OF INNER STRENGTH

Please record the following visualization on your device:

If you are listening to this as a recording, please close your eyes now and keep them closed throughout the visualization, until I tell you to open them.

Peace, peace, be still. Be still and be at peace. Peace, peace, be at peace. Be still and be at peace. Take a deep breath of divine love. Breathe in . . . and out . . . Take a deep breath of divine light. Breathe in . . . and out . . . Take a deep breath of forgiveness. Breathe in . . . and out . . . Take a big deep breath to go deeper. Breathe in . . . and out . . . Now relax and breathe normally.

Imagine you are standing on a mountaintop. You see a magnificent view in all directions. There are snow-capped peaks and green valleys.

The sky is deep cobalt blue, accented by pristine white lacy clouds. You feel a cool, clean, and fresh breeze. You have never felt such a feeling of inspiration, elation, and love for all of creation.

Verbalize the following affirmation audibly with inner strength and conviction:

I AM strong . . . I AM powerful . . . I AM invincible . . . My strength and power come from divine love . . . which pervades, permeates, and surrounds me . . . Love is my strength . . . Love is my power . . . Love is my glory . . . I AM a being of love . . . and my strength comes from . . . the overflowing love, joy, and happiness within me . . . I AM powerful because I AM love . . . Thank you, Spirit, and SO IT IS . . .

Now imagine a beauteous sphere of brilliant, pure white light of immeasurable glory above your head. It is the supreme light of Spirit. Now a dazzling ray of pure white light beams down from that sphere through the top of your head. It then streams down through your spine, which becomes perfectly aligned and radiant. As you stand straight and tall with confidence, the light begins to vibrate, radiate, and expand from within. This splendorous light now fills and surrounds your entire energy field, illuminating it with power and strength.

You are now encapsulated in a resplendent pillar of pure white light. This pillar of divine protection, which vibrates within and all around you, now fills you with safety, security, stability, invincibility, and unassailable might. You are an invincible being of light, free from fear, doubt, unworthiness, and failings, and filled with love, faith, trust, happiness, and success. You are divinely protected by the light of your being.

Now take a few moments of silence to enjoy the glorious, radiant pillar of light that surrounds you . . . [Record fifteen seconds of silence here.]

Then, with gratitude in your heart, keep your eyes closed as you come forth from the visualization and pretend you are blowing out four candles . . . [Record fifteen seconds of silence here.] Then, come all the way back to objective and subjective balance and open your eyes . . .

Now repeat the following affirmation audibly with your eyes open:

I AM alert . . . I AM awake . . . I AM very alert . . . I AM very awake . . . I AM objectively and subjectively balanced . . . I AM in control . . . I AM the only authority in my life . . . I AM divinely protected by the light of my being . . . Thank you, Spirit, and SO IT IS.

SELF-PROTECTION AFFIRMATION

To increase love, light, power, and divine protection in your energy field, speak this affirmation audibly with confidence and conviction. Speak as though your higher self is saying it through you:

The light of Spirit surrounds me.
The love of Spirit enfolds me.
The power of Spirit protects me.
The presence of Spirit watches over me.
Wherever I AM, Spirit is, and ALL IS WELL.

Take a few moments to write in your journal what you experienced by practicing the affirmations and visualizations in this chapter. Now that you've experienced inner strength, let's open the doorway to inner peace and contentment.

Chapter 6

Open the Doorway to Inner Peace and Contentment

Now it's time to take a deep dive into your higher self and become centered in the placid pool of serenity and contentment within. By going deep within to your center of being, you can experience inner peace and also radiate waves of peace to the environment.

INNER PEACE MEDITATION

Record the following meditation on your device:

If you are listening to this as a recording, please close your eyes now and keep them closed throughout the meditation, until I tell you to open them.

Peace, peace, be still. Be still and be at peace. Peace, peace, be at peace. Be still and be at peace. Perfect peace, perfect peace, perfect peace. Be still and be at peace. Take a deep breath of divine love.

Breathe in . . . and out . . . Take a deep breath of divine light. Breathe in . . . and out . . . Take a deep breath of relaxation. Breathe in . . . and out . . . Take a big deep breath to go deeper. Breathe in . . . and out . . . Now relax and breathe normally. Let go, let go, let go, let go, let go, let go, let God.

Breathe in . . . and out . . . Breathe normally and peacefully. Peace, peace, be still. Be still and be at peace. Take a big deep breath to go deeper. Breathe in . . . and out . . . Now breathe normally, easily, and effortlessly. Deeper, deeper, deeper into the wells of Spirit, into the silence of being. Relax, relax, release, and be at peace.

We now recognize that there is one power and one presence in the universe and in our lives—the omnipotent divine presence of perfect peace and tranquility. We are one with the power, the peace, quietude, serenity, tranquility, and contentment of this perfect presence now. We are one with the truth of our being, with the light of Spirit. One with wholeness, oneness, and pure consciousness.

We therefore claim the perfect, profound inner-peace meditation now that proceeds perfectly with divine order and timing. We now know that during this meditation you receive deep relaxation and serenity, as much as you can comfortably enjoy. You receive perfect wholeness, oneness, contentment, and deep inner peace. You now receive all that is wise to receive in this meditation—all that we have spoken or better. Thank you, Spirit, and SO IT IS.

Please repeat these affirmations audibly now:

I AM in control . . . I AM one with Spirit . . . I AM the only authority in my life . . . I AM divinely protected by the light of my being . . . I close off my aura and body of light to the lower levels of mind . . . and I open to the spiritual world . . .

The light of Spirit surrounds me . . . The love of Spirit enfolds me . . . The power of Spirit protects me . . . The presence of Spirit watches over me . . . Wherever I AM, Spirit is, and ALL IS WELL . . .

I invoke the divine presence . . . to eliminate any and all negations and limitations . . . that have prevented me . . . from experiencing inner peace . . . I now dispel all negations . . . of worry, doubt, fear . . . anxiety, frustration, agitation . . . confusion, limitation, unworthiness . . . anger, guilt, blame . . . sadness and pain . . . and any other thoughts and emotions . . . that no longer serve me . . . and that do not reflect the truth of my being . . . I now welcome and accept thoughts . . . of inner peace, love, certainty . . . strength, courage, happiness . . . serenity, tranquility, equipoise . . . equilibrium, balance, wholeness . . . contentment, trust, faith . . . ease and comfort . . . I AM now in control . . . I thank Spirit, and SO IT IS . . .

Now relax the mind and let go of the environment. Any sounds around you only serve to take you deeper into meditation. Release, loose, and let go of all cares and concerns of the day. Whatever limiting thoughts or negative beliefs you have brought into this meditation, now give them over to Spirit. Release these limitations and let go of them now as you take a big deep breath. Breathe in . . . and out . . . Then breathe normally.

Now become aware of your physical body . . . Anywhere you feel any sensation, tension, or stress, just allow your attention and awareness to simply rest on that place or places within the body that need healing. As you place attention on those sensations, take a few moments of quietude to allow them to dissipate . . . [Record thirty seconds of silence here.] Now take a deep breath to go deeper, deeper, into the wells of Spirit. Breathe in . . . and out . . . Then breathe normally.

Now become aware that your physical body is becoming very relaxed, quiet, and still. Every part of your body is becoming deeply relaxed. Take a big deep breath. Breathe in . . . and out . . . Then breathe normally . . . Now relax the eyes . . . the forehead . . . eyebrows . . . the space between the eyebrows . . . relax the head . . . the temples . . . cheeks . . . the jaw . . . neck relax . . . shoulders relax . . . upper arms . . . lower arms . . . relax the hands . . . the fingers . . .

Take a big deep breath. Breathe in . . . and out . . . Then breathe normally and relax the chest . . . the stomach . . . the upper back . . .

lower back . . . buttocks . . . thighs . . . Take a big deep breath. Breathe in . . . and out . . . Then breathe normally and relax the knees . . . the legs . . . ankles . . . the feet . . . toes . . . the forehead relax . . . eyebrows relax . . . relax the space between the eyebrows . . .

Now take a big deep breath to relax your whole body. Breathe in . . . and out . . . Take another big deep breath to fill up the entire body with peace. Breathe in . . . and out . . . Then breathe easily and normally. Completely let go and relax . . . Peace, peace, be still. Be still and be at peace . . .

Now become aware of your conscious mind as you take a big deep breath to go deeper. Breathe in . . . and out . . . Then breathe normally and effortlessly. As your body settles down to deep relaxation, your conscious mind settles down to complete quietude . . . As your breathing becomes refined and subtle, your mind becomes serene and tranquil, like a still pond, without a ripple . . . Now take a big deep breath to go even deeper into that silence. Breathe in . . . and out . . . Then breathe easily and normally. Peace, peace, be still. Be still and be at peace . . .

Now allow your attention to drift into the subconscious realm, where your mind rests in deep silence and peace, like the water at the bottom of the ocean—deep and quiet, in perfect calm and serenity . . . Your mind is absorbed in that total stillness, at the depth of that silent ocean. Take a big deep breath and go deeper, deeper, into the wells of Spirit. Breathe in . . . and out . . . Then breathe normally and easily. Peace, peace, be still . . . Be still, and be at peace.

Now take another deep breath. Breathe in . . . and out . . . Breathe normally and peacefully. Now become aware of the seeming veil that has separated you from Spirit. Take a big deep breath to glide effortlessly through that veil and traverse into the realm of Spirit. Breathe in . . . and out . . . And again breathe in . . . and out . . . Then breathe normally.

Cross through that seeming veil and then welcome the divine presence of Spirit into your being. Open your heart to receive the perfect peace and tranquility that flood into your being. Feel the waves of deep relaxation and relief that come from letting go and allowing yourself to plunge into the perfect stillness, harmony, and equanimity of Spirit.

Now take another deep breath. Breathe in . . . and out . . . Then breathe normally. Let go and let Spirit take you deeper, deeper still, into the wells of Spirit, into the silence of being . . . Peace, peace, be still . . . Relax, relax, release, and be at peace. Relax, let go, and give up completely. Give up everything to Spirit as you allow your awareness to dive into the absolute perfection of being. Beyond the realm of duality, now transcend into the nameless, formless, quality-less, motionless, imperishable absolute, one without a second, beyond duality.

Now take a deep breath and ask Spirit to take you deeper, into the realm of silence, absolute bliss consciousness, at the center of being. Breathe in . . . and out . . . And again breathe in . . . and out . . . Then breathe normally. Once you've attained this state of inner peace and deep relaxation, that's the time to simply let go and remain in quietude.

You may stay there for a few seconds, for a minute, or several minutes. There's no time in the timeless. You might notice your awareness resting in the state of *samadhi*—equipoise of mind and stillness of body.

Your breathing may become quiet and still, until you're barely breathing at all. Your heart might slow down. Your body might feel numb, transparent, or even vanished. Deeply absorbed in your higher self, you may forget your body and surroundings.

Now take a couple of deep breaths and remain in silence for a few minutes. Breathe in . . . and out . . . And another deep breath. Breathe in . . . and out . . . Now breathe normally. If, at any time, you feel you're getting out of the silence, just take a deep breath to go back into stillness . . . [Record three minutes of silence here.]

Peace, peace be still. Be still and be at peace. Perfect peace, perfect peace, perfect peace. Be still and be at peace. Now that you've experienced inner peace and contentment in your higher self, it's time to give gratitude and come out of meditation.

Please keep your eyes closed until I tell you to open them. With gratitude in your heart, lean forward very slightly in your chair. Then take a big deep breath, and as you exhale, pretend you're quickly, vigorously blowing out a candle.

Take a deep breath like this right now, and pretend you're blowing out a candle . . . Then take a second deep breath and blow out another candle . . . Become aware of your mind, knowing the mind is one with

Spirit, one with the truth of being. The mind is now united with divine mind, and every thought is a divine revelation and inspiration.

Take another big deep breath and blow out another candle . . . Now become aware of your physical body . . . The body has been permanently transformed and lifted by this meditation. The physical body is one with the divine body and is transmuted into a radiant body of pure light, brilliance, splendor, and magnificence, in robust health and well-being.

Now take another big deep breath and blow out a candle as you become aware of the environment, yet still keeping your eyes closed . . . Become aware of your body sitting in the chair, the space around you, coming back to this time and place. Know that you bring into the environment all you have gained from this meditation. As you move into daily life, you vibrate with the divine presence and radiate it all around you each moment of each day. You are a brilliant being of light. You are a walking, talking, breathing, living vessel of Spirit, and you realize the magnificence of your being.

Now take four deep, vigorous breaths and blow out four candles . . . Then come all the way back to objective and subjective balance and open your eyes . . .

Now repeat the following affirmation audibly while keeping your eyes open:

I AM alert . . . I AM awake . . . I AM very alert . . . I AM very awake . . . I AM objectively and subjectively balanced . . . I AM in control . . . I AM the only authority in my life . . . I AM divinely protected by the light of my being . . . Thank you, Spirit, and SO IT IS.

Be sure to make a note in your journal about the experience of inner peace you enjoyed during this meditation. Now we will move on to the next section of the book, where you'll illuminate your everyday life, first by opening the doorway to meaningful relationships.

Part II

Illuminating Your Everyday Life

Chapter 7

Open the Doorway to Meaningful Relationships

In this chapter you'll practice affirmations that help you create greater harmony and depth in family relationships, greater communication and concord at work, supportive and loyal friendships, and compatible love partnerships.

HEALING FAMILIAL RELATIONSHIPS

To heal your relationship with your family, say this affirmation audibly in a confident, clear, empowering voice, as though your higher self is speaking the words through you:

I now call upon Spirit to bring harmony, peace, and love into my family. I now recognize there is one power and one presence in the universe and in my life—the divine Spirit. This spiritual presence is the essence of pure, unconditional love. I AM now merged with and one with this divine presence in a seamless unified wholeness. There is no separation between Spirit and me. Therefore I AM the pure unconditional love that Spirit is.

I now therefore know and claim that my family is filled with peace, harmony, love, joy, and camaraderie, and my attitude about my family members is compassionate, forgiving, tolerant, accepting, and permissive.

I no longer hold grudges and harbor resentment towards family members. I let go of any idea that I have been slighted or wronged. No matter what family members have done or failed to do in the past, I now let go of all negative attitudes I have held against them.

I know holding on to negative emotions hurts no one other than myself. It poisons my self-esteem and destroys my well-being. Therefore, I now let go of all negative feelings about family members. I now put all these harmful, toxic feelings into a big gunnysack and hand it over to Spirit. I now let go and let Spirit fill me with love, peace, harmony, happiness, forgiveness, healing, and contentment. I welcome into my life warm, supportive, loving familial relationships right now.

I now accept fully in consciousness that I am healed of all old encrusted beliefs, habits, and conditions that no longer serve me. I now walk into the light of Spirit in great joy and fulfillment. My family members are now safe, secure, loved, and filled with life. And I AM enjoying loving, harmonious, peaceful relationships with my family now.

I now give gratitude to Spirit for this healing. Thank you, Spirit, and SO BE IT.

ENHANCING WORK RELATIONSHIPS

Please say this affirmation audibly in a confident, clear, empowering voice:

I call upon Spirit to cut any and all binding ties and karmic bonds between my coworkers and me. These binding ties are now lovingly cut, cut, cut, cut, cut, cut, cut, cut, cut, cut, cut, cut, cut, cut, lifted, loved, healed, released, dissolved, and completely let go into the light of divine love and truth.

Any and all negative energies in my workplace are now lifted into the light of divine love and truth. All disharmony, infighting, back-biting, jealousy, inequality, competition, gender inequity, and cliquishness are now lovingly lifted, healed, released, dissolved, and let go into the light of divine truth, and they are gone. Now my workplace is filled with harmony, acceptance, tolerance, love, compassion, justice, fairness, prosperity, abundance, happiness, gratitude, and inclusiveness.

I now declare that true love ties are established between all my coworkers and me. I know that unconditional love, harmony, and happiness fill my workplace, now.

I now call forth Holy Spirit, Saint Germaine, Master Jesus, Babaji, Archangel Michael, the angels and archangels, and divine light beings who come in the name of God to fill my workplace with divine love and light. I ask these divine beings to lift the atmosphere in my workplace. The vibration of my workplace is now lifted, lifted, lifted, lifted, lifted, lifted, lifted, lifted, lifted into a divine vibration of pure love and light.

The workplace is now filled, permeated, and surrounded with peace, love, and happiness. I enjoy harmonious, rewarding relationships with my coworkers now. All is well in the workplace now. Thank you, Spirit, and SO IT IS.

MAKING LASTING FRIENDSHIPS

Say this affirmation audibly in a confident, clear, empowering voice:

I now call upon Spirit to bring into my life compatible lifelong friendships with people of like mind. I now welcome and accept into my life wonderful friends who are attuned with me in every way—mentally, emotionally, spiritually, morally, and socially. I now attract new friends who share similar likes, interests, appetites, ideals, and values.

I now release from my mind and from my life any and all people who are incompatible with me, and who distract me from my true life path and purpose. I let go of all people who do not support me in reaching my heartfelt desires and meaningful goals.

I now attract friends who are supportive, loyal, healing, loving, comforting, caring, helpful, patient, gentle, compassionate, joyful, fun, uplifting, empowering, and wise. My friends are there for me when I need them. They are trustworthy, honest, and upright. They show that they care and they have my best interests at heart.

I now welcome into my life loyal and loving friends who stay with me through thick and thin. I now accept fully in consciousness all that I have spoken, or better. I thank Spirit that this is so, and SO IT IS.

ATTRACTING A SOUL MATE

Say this affirmation audibly in a confident, clear, empowering voice.

I now call upon Spirit to bring my perfect partner into my life who is compatible and harmonious with me on every level—physically, mentally, emotionally, spiritually, sexually, socially, and financially, and with whom I have similar likes, interests, appetites, ideals, values, and morals.

I now know this perfect partner is attractive to me and attracted to me on every level. This partner is loving, loyal, caring, helpful, patient, gentle, compassionate, joyful, fun, uplifting, empowering, wise, honest, upright, and emotionally supportive. I love my partner and I also like my partner, because there is ease, comfort, and harmony between us. Our relationship is without drama, contention, competition, discord, or struggle. There is love, friendship, support, and effortlessness.

I now release from my mind any and all feelings that have blocked me from my perfect partnership now. I now let go of thoughts of unworthiness, self-sabotage, self-hatred, and self-condemnation. These thoughts are now released into the light of Spirit and burnt in the fire of divine love.

I now welcome into my life powerful thoughts of self-worth, self-love, self-empowerment, and self-acceptance. I like myself. I love myself. I accept myself. I AM worthy to attract love into my life. I AM loved. I AM love.

Not only do I pray to attract my perfect partner, but I also take time to meet like-minded people. I place myself in situations and events where I mingle with new people, and I make efforts in the direction of finding a compatible partner in the physical world.

I now give gratitude for my perfect partner coming into my life now. I accept fully in consciousness all that I have spoken, or better. I thank Spirit that this is so now, and SO IT IS.

Be sure to make a note in your journal about how these affirmations are improving your relationships. In the next chapter we'll open the doorway to a purposeful, authentic life.

Chapter 8

Open the Doorway to a Purposeful, Authentic Life

There's one question that I find people ask me again and again: "What is my life purpose?" This chapter can help you discover your divine purpose, find your true self, and live your life authentically and genuinely.

UNLIMITED THINKING EXERCISE

This is going to be a "writing meditation." Please get out a piece of paper and a pen and get ready to write.

On your paper, please write a list of what you would do with your life, day by day, if you knew that you could never fail, and that you had unlimited time, perfect health, unlimited energy, unlimited money, unlimited mobility, unlimited courage, unlimited optimism, unlimited joy, unlimited strength, unlimited self-confidence, unlimited enthusiasm, unlimited persistence and perseverance, unlimited access to anyone you want to work with, as many helpers and assistants as you would ever want or need, and you could pay them any salary because you have unlimited funds.

Please don't write how you would spend your money and what cars, mansions, and other toys you would buy. Instead, please write a list of what you would do with your time each day. When you get up in the morning, what would you do? Whom would you meet? How would you spend your days? What endeavors would you engage in? What goals would you fulfill? Remember that in this unlimited scenario, you can do *anything,* and it's impossible for you to fail.

Do not read the next paragraph until you've completed writing your list. Please do that now.

Now that you've finished writing your list, please look it over. What you have written is a powerful, life-transforming document. From the perspective of unlimited thinking, you've uncovered your true heart's desires and soul's longings. You've created a blueprint for the rest of your life. Even though you might feel the visions on your list are impossible to achieve, the reality is they came from the depths of your soul, and, in fact, they are possible. Anything is possible with faith.

You can pick just one vision on your list, set an intention to create it, and begin to take baby steps towards achieving it. When you start taking those steps, nature comes along and supports you to attain that vision. You already have everything you need within you to fulfill your destiny. Just begin now.

Keep this paper in a safe place and revisit it often to see how many of the visions that you've written on your list have manifested in your life.

FINDING YOUR GENUINE SELF

Who are you? How can you discover who you really are and what you're doing on this planet? Meditation is a way to experience your true self. Here's a meditation to help you do that. Please record this meditation on your device:

If you are listening to this as a recording, please close your eyes now and keep them closed throughout the meditation, until I tell you to open them.

Peace, peace, be still. Be still and be at peace. Peace, peace, be at peace. Be still and be at peace. Perfect peace, perfect peace, perfect peace. Be still and be at peace. Take a deep breath of divine love. Breathe in . . . and out . . . Take a deep breath of divine light. Breathe in . . . and out . . . Take a deep breath of relaxation. Breathe in . . . and out . . . Take a big deep breath to go deeper. Breathe in . . . and out . . . Relax, relax, release. Release and be at peace. Now completely let go and breathe normally.

I now call upon Spirit to take you into a profound experience of your higher self. I ask that you be taken deeper, into your inner being, which is your true self. Let go, let go, let go, let go. Let go, let go, let God. Trust that you are going deep within, into the silence of being, into your own inner divinity.

Dear, beautiful being of light, you are not who you think you are. You have believed yourself to be something you are not. You are not the body you inhabit. You are not the color of your skin. You are not the mind thinking endless thoughts. You are not your past. You are not your regrets. You are not your successes. You are not your failures. You are not your story. You are not your excuses. You are not the clothing you wear. You are not your bank account. You are not your home or your car. You are not your profession. You are not your talents. You are not your parents or your children. You are not your religion. You are not your beliefs. You are not your situation. You are not your circumstances. You are not a citizen of any city, state, province, or country. You are not a member of the human population. You are not a human being inhabiting the earth.

You are not who you think you are. For you are not the ego, you are not the intellect, and you are not what you call "I." Though thoughts flash into your mind like pictures onto a cinema screen, those pictures are not who you are. For your true Self is the screen and not the pictures. When the pictures overshadow the screen, it becomes hidden. But behind the pictures is the screen, and without the screen, no pictures exist.

Though clay jars contain a volume of air within them, when you break the jars, what remains? Only air. The air in the jar becomes one with the air everywhere. The air within the jar was always the same as the air outside the jar. Similarly, you are one with your true nature of being, which is present everywhere. There is no separation between you and all that is present in the cosmos.

You are not who you think you are. Though you believe yourself to be separate, you are one with Spirit. You are the unbounded, infinite, imperishable, unborn, undying, eternal, omniscient, omnipresent, omnipotent, absolute pure consciousness, without beginning or end. You are the alpha and the omega. You are the ouroboros, the snake eating its own tail, the "all is one."

You are much more magnificent, radiant, and beauteous than you could ever imagine. You shine like a million suns and vibrate with light, love, joy, peace, harmony, oneness, wholeness, and fulfillment. Through your free will, you can do anything.

What will you do with the power you possess? What will you do with the few precious breaths you take while walking this planet? You have the power to make every moment meaningful. So make a choice now to do what you love, and do something that makes a difference. Now take a few moments to consider what you will do with the rest of your time in this body. What will you learn? What are your unique gifts, talents, and attributes that you will contribute? Make an inner commitment now to do what you are here on earth to do . . . [Record one minute of silence here.]

Now, with gratitude in your heart, keep your eyes closed as you come forth from the meditation and pretend you are blowing out four candles . . . [Record fifteen seconds of silence here.] Then, come all the way back to objective and subjective balance and open your eyes . . .

Now repeat the following affirmation audibly with your eyes open:

I AM alert . . . I AM awake . . . I AM very alert . . . I AM very awake . . . I AM objectively and subjectively balanced . . . I AM in control . . . I AM the only authority in my life . . . I AM divinely protected by the light of my being . . . Thank you, Spirit, and SO IT IS.

LIVING LIFE AUTHENTICALLY

Your life can be joyful and meaningful when you live authentically and are willing to show your genuine feelings, desires, and needs. This affirmation can help you do that. Say it audibly with confidence and conviction.

I AM that I AM.
I AM light. I AM love. I AM real.
I AM my true self. I AM exactly who I AM.
I never hide behind any mask or veneer.

I AM my real self—genuine and authentic.
I AM complete, whole, and fulfilled, now and always.
Nothing and no one can make me less than I AM.
I now stand in the light of Spirit—invincible and unassailable.
I AM the truth. I AM the good. I AM the glory. I AM life.
I AM perfection everywhere now.
I AM perfection here now.
Thank you, Spirit, and SO IT IS.

Be sure to make a note in your journal about what you learned and how you benefited from practicing the exercises and meditations in this chapter. Now in the next chapter, we'll open the doorway to perfect health and unlimited energy.

Chapter 9

Open the Doorway to Health and Energy

By practicing the visualizations and meditations in this chapter, you can gain greater energy, improve your health, and increase your well-being. Please note these methods are not cures to diseases, and no medical claim is made about their efficacy. Consult a medical professional before practicing any methods in this book.

HEALING AND ENERGIZING YOUR BODY

Please record the following on your device:

If you are listening to this as a recording, please close your eyes now and keep them closed throughout the visualization, until I tell you to open them.

Peace, peace, be still. Be still and be at peace. Peace, peace, be at peace. Be still and be at peace. Perfect peace, perfect peace, perfect

peace. Be still and be at peace. Take a deep breath of divine love. Breathe in . . . and out . . . Take a deep breath of divine light. Breathe in . . . and out . . . Take a deep breath of relaxation. Breathe in . . . and out . . . Let go, let go, let go, let go. Let go, let go, let God. Now relax and breathe normally.

We now call forth the divine beings of light who come in the name of God to assist in this healing meditation. Now imagine you are lying on your back on the most comfortable bed. You are completely relaxed. Archangel Raphael, the celestial healer, is standing to the right of the bed, facing your body. Envision that Raphael receives directly from Spirit a healing instrument that he now uses to spray a crystalline clear, restorative, cleansing, miraculous, healing liquid with anti-inflammatory, antibacterial, and antiviral properties.

Raphael now sprays this warm, pure, comforting liquid of perfect temperature throughout your subtle and physical bodies, both inside and out. All dross and debris are washed away from your cells. All toxic thoughts and emotions are removed from your subtle body. All vestiges of darkness are lifted into the pure light of Spirit and burnt to ashes in the fire of divine love.

Now Raphael uses another celestial instrument to wash pure, pristine, warm aquifer water of perfect temperature throughout your subtle and physical bodies, both inside and out, which removes any remaining physical and mental toxins. Your body is now cleansed, healed, beauteous, sparkling, and perfect—inside and out.

Raphael now uses a third celestial instrument that sprays a mist of perfect robust health, perfect well-being, divine love, light, joy, freedom, prosperity, fulfillment, and contentment throughout your subtle and physical bodies, both inside and out. Your cells are now restored, and all systems in your body function perfectly.

You are now dried off and clothed in pure white garments, and you take a seat in the most comfortable padded recliner. Saint Germaine appears before you and blazes his violet, consuming, purifying flame throughout every atom of your body, cleansing, purifying, and elevating your spiritual energy. Your energy is now lifted to the highest vibrational octave you can possibly comfortably enjoy.

The Holy Spirit, the Spirit of truth and wholeness, now brings forth her clear white light and white fire, infusing your body with purity, wholeness, and oneness. Master Jesus now fills your body with a beauteous golden, radiant Christ consciousness light, which permeates and surrounds every cell, lighting up, energizing, and bringing wellness to every molecule. See that shining golden light pervading your body now.

Please repeat this affirmation now in a strong, powerful voice:

I AM filled with the purity of divine love . . . I AM filled with divine, radiant light . . . I AM filled with robust health and well-being . . . I AM filled with energy, enthusiasm, and love of life . . . I AM restored, happy, whole, and filled with health and vigor . . . Thank you, Spirit, and SO IT IS . . .

Then, with gratitude in your heart, keep your eyes closed as you come forth from the visualization and pretend you are blowing out four candles . . . [Record fifteen seconds of silence here.] Then, come all the way back to objective and subjective balance and open your eyes . . .

Now repeat the following affirmation audibly with your eyes open:

I AM alert . . . I AM awake . . . I AM very alert . . . I AM very awake . . . I AM objectively and subjectively balanced . . . I AM in control . . . I AM the only authority in my life . . . I AM divinely protected by the light of my being . . . Thank you, Spirit, and SO IT IS.

FREEDOM FROM PAIN

Anytime you feel pain in the body, this meditation is a powerful solution that has proven highly effective time after time. This meditation is not a cure and should not be construed as medical advice. It is not a replacement for medication. Be sure to consult your health professional before embarking on any meditation program.

Please record the following meditation on your device:

If you are listening to this as a recording, please close your eyes now and keep them closed throughout the meditation, until I tell you to open them.

Peace, peace, be still. Be still and be at peace. Peace, peace, be at peace. Be still and be at peace. Perfect peace, perfect peace, perfect peace. Be still and be at peace. Take a deep breath of divine love. Breathe in . . . and out . . . Take a deep breath of divine light. Breathe in . . . and out . . . Take a deep breath of relaxation. Breathe in . . . and out . . . Take a big deep breath to go deeper. Breathe in . . . and out.

Let go, let go, let go, let go. Let go, let go, let God. Now relax and breathe normally.

Allow yourself to be at peace. Feel your body melting into the chair or whatever you are sitting on. Take a few deep breaths now, and with every out-breath, let yourself just give up all you've been holding on to . . . [Record thirty seconds of silence here.] The pain in your body is a cry for help. Pain is the natural way the body signals you when it wants your attention. Now you will give the body what it needs—your attention. Take a big deep breath of relaxation. Breathe in . . . and out . . . Let go, let go, let go, let go. Let go, let go, let God. Now relax fully and breathe normally.

Now just let go and rest your attention gently on your body. You might notice some sensations of pain or other sensations drawing your attention. Now just quietly place your attention on the place or places within your body where you notice those sensations. As you place your attention on the sensations, do not attempt to "heal" the sensations, "reduce" the sensations, or "manipulate" the sensations. Instead, just quietly and lovingly rest your attention on the sensations.

Rather than resisting sensations or labeling sensations as "pain," instead simply notice they are nothing more than sensations. Consider them to just be sensations. Now imagine you are diving right into the middle of the sensations rather than resisting them. Dive right into the sensations and allow yourself to quietly feel them, without resistance.

As you continue to place your attention on the sensations, they will tend to dissipate. Just place your attention there quietly. Do not resist, but just dive right in now and silently feel the sensations for a few minutes and notice how they dissipate . . . [Record three minutes of silence here.]

Then, with gratitude in your heart, keep your eyes closed as you come forth from the meditation and pretend you are blowing out four candles . . . [Record fifteen seconds of silence here.] Then, come all the way back to objective and subjective balance and open your eyes . . .

Now repeat the following affirmation audibly with your eyes open:

I AM alert . . . I AM awake . . . I AM very alert . . . I AM very awake . . . I AM objectively and subjectively balanced . . . I AM in control . . . I AM the only authority in my life . . . I AM divinely protected by the light of my being . . . Thank you, Spirit, and SO IT IS.

Before moving on into the next chapter, please make a note in your journal describing your experiences of the practices you learned in this chapter. In the next chapter, you'll open the doorway to meaningful abundance and prosperity.

Chapter 10

Open the Doorway to Meaningful Abundance

This chapter can help you tap into the source of prosperity, attract money and blessings, and achieve real wealth—the abundance of Spirit. The steps to affluence are the same as achieving any other goal: 1) resolute decision, 2) positive intention, 3) laser-sharp focus of attention, and 4) unfailing persistence.

TAPPING THE SOURCE OF PROSPERITY

Please record the following visualization on your device:

If you are listening to this as a recording, please close your eyes now and keep them closed throughout the meditation, until I tell you to open them.

Peace, peace, be still. Be still and be at peace. Peace, peace, be at peace. Be still and be at peace. Perfect peace, perfect peace, perfect

peace. Be still and be at peace. Take a deep breath of divine love. Breathe in . . . and out . . . Take a deep breath of divine light. Breathe in . . . and out . . . Take a deep breath of relaxation. Breathe in . . . and out . . . Now relax and breathe normally. Let go, let go, let go, let go. Let go, let go, let God.

Imagine a beauteous goddess of wealth standing before you. She is standing on a lotus flower and dressed in a scarlet gown with spun gold bordering her garment. She has long, flowing, brunette locks, and she wears a golden crown bedecked with precious jewels, a gem-encrusted golden necklace, and golden bracelets and anklets. A garland of fragrant jasmine flowers encircles her neck. Her countenance is peaceful and radiates bliss.

This goddess, whose name is Lakshmi, now smiles upon you, and her glance bestows divine grace and energy. You can feel her blessings wash over you, and you are cleansed, lifted, and healed by the energy she emits from her large, sparkling, ebony eyes.

This luminous goddess is a never-ending source of gold coins, which she begins to bestow upon you. Coins are now falling from her hands and into your energy field. A perpetual stream of gold coins now flows from her hands into your energy field, and you are receiving this endless stream of money, prosperity, and bounty. You are now open to receive all the wealth that Lakshmi is bestowing upon you, continually and perpetually.

Now repeat this affirmation audibly in a clear and convincing voice:

I AM money . . . I AM wealth . . .
I AM one with . . . the unlimited source of all that is . . .
Boundless is the divine substance . . . this universe is made of . . .
I now tap into . . . that unlimited universal source . . .
I now receive . . . unlimited wealth, money, and prosperity . . .
Thank you, Spirit, and SO IT IS. . .

Then, with gratitude in your heart, come forth from this visualization by taking at least four deep vigorous breaths and pretend you are blowing out four candles . . . [Record fifteen seconds of silence here.] Then, come all the way back to objective and subjective balance and open your eyes . . .

Now speak the following affirmation audibly with your eyes open:

I AM alert . . . I AM awake . . . I AM very alert . . . I AM very
awake . . . I AM objectively and subjectively balanced . . . I AM in
control . . . I AM the only authority in my life . . . I AM divinely
protected by the light of my being . . . Thank you, Spirit, and SO
IT IS.

RECEIVING THE BLESSINGS OF SPIRIT

When you appreciate all the blessings you have in your life and you expect unwaveringly to receive even more, then Spirit's gifts flow into your life in an endless stream. This affirmation can help you receive perpetual abundance. Say this affirmation audibly, clearly, and with conviction:

I now open my heart to Spirit.
My life is blessed with ever-increasing waves of grace.
I thank Spirit for all the bounty in my life.
I AM thankful for my life, my health, and my constant beating heart.
I thank Spirit for my home, my family, and friends.
I AM grateful for my work and my coworkers.
I thank Spirit for all the blessings, both materially and spiritually.
I AM grateful for my spiritual connection.
I AM grateful for divine protection, safety, and security.
I give gratitude for my higher self, filled with bliss.
I AM grateful for my inner source of unlimited energy and wisdom.
I thank Spirit that I AM one with Spirit.
Thank you, Spirit, and SO BE IT.

ACHIEVING TRUE WEALTH

Please record the following meditation on your device:

If you are listening to this as a recording, please close your eyes now and keep them closed throughout the meditation, until I tell you to open them.

Peace, peace, be still. Be still and be at peace. Peace, peace, be at peace. Be still and be at peace. Perfect peace, perfect peace, perfect peace. Be still and be at peace. Take a deep breath of divine love. Breathe in . . . and out . . . Take a deep breath of divine light. Breathe in . . . and out . . . Take a deep breath of relaxation. Breathe in . . . and out . . . Now relax and breathe normally. Let go, let go, let go, let go. Let go, let go, let God.

We now know that there is one power, one presence, and one divine substance in the universe and in our lives. That divine substance is unlimited wealth and abundance, because it is the source of everything in the cosmos. Divine substance is unbounded, replete, and never-ending. There is nothing lacking in divine substance. It is free and available for everyone now and always.

We are now one with that divine, all-powerful, all-encompassing substance of unlimited wealth and abundance. We are complete and whole now. Nothing is lacking, and all is available for the taking.

We now therefore know and claim that you are divinely provided for, eternally, without limit. You are blessed with abundance, wealth, and prosperity. Release from your mind all feelings of lack and deficiency now. Let go of all thoughts of inadequacy, unworthiness, loss, shortfalls, and poverty. Such negative thoughts and feelings are now lifted, healed, released, and let go, and they are gone. They are burnt to ashes in the fire of divine love. Now accept and welcome into your mind new, positive, life-supporting thoughts of self-acceptance, self-worth, gain, profit, wealth, prosperity, and abundance.

Release from your mind any false beliefs that spiritual people are supposed to be poor and that rich people cannot enter the kingdom of heaven. Know now that the kingdom of heaven is open to rich and poor alike, and all are invited to receive the bounty of heavenly love and blessings.

Open your heart now to receive the infinite light of divine love. You are worthy to receive the benevolence of Spirit. You are blessed and beloved of Spirit. You are a radiant being of light, living in the heart of divine love. Open to receive pure love, pure light, and the never-ending generosity of Spirit. All of Spirit's blessings are here for the taking. Open to receive. Let the bounty of Spirit flood into your being. Open to all that Spirit has in store for you. Let go of all blocks to the flow of infinite abundance. Welcome and embrace prosperity now.

Now, with gratitude in your heart, come forth from this visualization by taking at least four deep vigorous breaths and pretend you are blowing out four candles . . . [Record fifteen seconds of silence here.] Then, come all the way back to objective and subjective balance and open your eyes . . .

Now speak the following affirmation audibly with your eyes wide open:

> *I AM alert . . . I AM awake . . . I AM very alert . . . I AM very awake . . . I AM objectively and subjectively balanced . . . I AM in control . . . I AM the only authority in my life . . . I AM divinely protected by the light of my being . . . Thank you Spirit, and SO IT IS.*

Be sure to make a note in your journal about what you learned from the exercises and meditations you practiced in this chapter. Now in the next chapter, we'll open the doorway to true power and genuine success.

Chapter 11

Open the Doorway to Real Power and True Success

In this chapter you'll practice meditations and affirmations that can help you achieve your heart's desires and attain true empowerment, the power that arises from within when you express who you really are—your genuine self.

EXPRESSING YOUR TRUE SELF

Say this affirmation audibly in a powerful voice with conviction and certainty:

> *I AM in control. I AM the only authority in my life. I AM the expression of my true nature of being. I AM powerful, strong, and mighty, and I walk my own pathway with conviction in my purpose. I fulfill my destiny.*

I call upon Spirit to help me release, loose, and let go of anything preventing me from expressing my true self. I now release all negative thoughts and emotions that no longer serve me. I let go of feelings of doubt, guilt, unworthiness, timidity, self-sabotage, fear of shame, fear of exposure, and fear of making mistakes. These negative feelings are now lifted, healed, released, and let go into the light of divine truth and love. And they are gone.

I now rise above all these limiting ideas, emotions, concepts, and feelings. I now welcome into my life new, positive, creative thoughts of absolute faith in Spirit, absolute trust in myself, conviction in my self-worth, indomitable courage, resolute self-confidence, boldness, perseverance, endurance, persistency, steadfastness, and tenacity.

I AM now filled with determination to be myself and express my truth now. Nothing and no one stands in my way as I define my own pathway and walk it with courage. I AM a mighty being of light, and I express my talents and gifts right now.

I now give gratitude to Spirit for helping me to be myself and to step into my true power. I now let go and let Spirit take the reins of my life and lead me into divine grace and glory. I now release this affirmation into the Spiritual Law, knowing that it does manifest now in perfect ways. Thank you, Spirit, and SO IT IS.

DIVINE MOTHER MANTRA

The Devi Mantra, an invocation of the goddess Durga, the Supreme Mother, is used by millions of people in India. It is one of the most powerful mantras to help you achieve success and to develop spiritual abilities. It improves concentration, intelligence, and academic performance. It bestows courage, energy, and self-confidence, and thereby helps you fulfill your desires. It defeats negative energy, stress, and depression, and increases vitality, strength, happiness, and harmonious relationships. It removes fear and protects you from enemies and evil intentions.

Please say or chant this mantra audibly in a clear voice, with conviction. You can also use the mantra silently and repeat it 108 times for great benefit:

Om Aim Hreem Kleem Chamundaye Viche

Please learn how to pronounce the mantra before trying to recite or repeat it. There are several online videos where you can watch, listen, and learn how. The Spiritual India channel on You Tube offers excellent videos. You can find them by searching the Spiritual India channel for the mantra "Om Aim Hreem Kleem Chamundaye Viche."

While chanting mantras, people often use a rosary called a *mala* to count the number of repetitions, as it is generally recommended to chant mantras 108 times. Therefore *rudraksha* (a seed holy to Lord Shiva) or sandalwood malas are strung with 108 beads.

SUCCESS MAGNET MEDITATION

Please record the following meditation on your device:

If you are listening to this as a recording, please close your eyes now and keep them closed throughout the meditation, until I tell you to open them.

Peace, peace, be still. Be still and be at peace. Peace, peace, be at peace. Be still and be at peace. Perfect peace, perfect peace, perfect peace. Be still and be at peace. Take a deep breath of divine love. Breathe in . . . and out . . . Take a deep breath of divine light. Breathe in . . . and out . . . Take a deep breath of relaxation. Breathe in . . . and out . . . Now relax and breathe normally. Let go, let go, let go, let go, let go, let go, let God.

Imagine now that you are a success magnet. You lead a charmed life. You now sail through life with ease and comfort, without drama and hardship. Your life is filled with love, happiness, friends, family, and fulfillment. You are thankful for all your blessings. You are healthy, prosperous, and accomplished. You are content with your life and it flows naturally.

Imagine your relationships with friends, family, and coworkers are effortless and easy. Your love life is happy and fulfilling. Your work life is relaxed, secure, joyous, and you enjoy what you do day by day. You feel satisfied that what you are doing makes a difference. Your life is lived in *dharma* rather than drama.

Your real success is not counted by the money in your pocket or in your bank account. The real treasure and measure of your success is deep within your own heart. Success comes not because you are an interesting, fascinating person. Success comes to you because you are an interested, fascinated person. You are successful because of your interest, fascination, and love of people around you.

Now repeat this affirmation audibly in a powerful voice:

I AM a success magnet . . . I AM successful because I AM happy . . . Happiness does not come to me . . . because of my success . . . Success comes to me now . . . because I am joyful and happy within . . . My success is not measured in money . . . It is measured by the real treasures within . . . It is measured by the love and joy . . . that I find within my heart . . . and that I radiate . . . from the center of my being . . . My true success comes . . . when I see the smiles . . . upon the faces of people . . . that I lift and inspire . . . through my words and deeds . . . I AM a success magnet . . . because I radiate what real success is . . . I radiate joy, happiness, and fulfillment . . .

Now spend a few moments counting all the small successes you've had today and give gratitude to Spirit for all the success you have in your life . . . [Record thirty seconds of silence here.]

Then, with deep gratitude in your heart, keep your eyes closed as you come forth from the meditation and pretend you are blowing out four candles . . . [Record fifteen seconds of silence here.] Then, come all the way back to objective and subjective balance and open your eyes . . .

Now repeat the following affirmation audibly with your eyes open:

I AM alert . . . I AM awake . . . I AM very alert . . . I AM very awake . . . I AM objectively and subjectively balanced . . . I AM in control . . . I AM the only authority in my life . . . I AM divinely protected by the light of my being . . . Thank you, Spirit, and SO IT IS.

Please make a note in your journal about what you experienced from practicing the affirmations and meditations in this chapter. Now in the next section, we'll begin to illuminate the planet and open the doorway to universal love.

Part III

Illuminating the Planet

Chapter 12

Open the Doorway to Universal Love

Your thoughts, words, and deeds affect not only yourself. They also extend their reach to touch all of humanity. This chapter can help you transform the planet from a struggle of intolerance, prejudice, bigotry, bias, partisanship, and divisiveness into a paradise of universal harmony and love for all beings.

PLANETARY LOVE RADIATION

Please record the following meditation on your device:

If you are listening to this as a recording, please close your eyes now and keep them closed throughout the meditation, until I tell you to open them.

Peace, peace, be still. Be still and be at peace. Peace, peace, be at peace. Be still and be at peace. Perfect peace, perfect peace, perfect

peace. Be still and be at peace. Take a deep breath of divine love. Breathe in . . . and out . . . Take a deep breath of divine light. Breathe in . . . and out . . . Take a deep breath of relaxation. Breathe in . . . and out . . . Take a big deep breath to go deeper. Breathe in . . . and out . . . Deeper, deeper, deeper into the wells of Spirit, into the silence of being. Now relax and breathe normally.

Breathe in . . . and out . . . Then breathe normally and peacefully. Relax, relax, release, and be at peace. Let go and be at peace. Take a big deep breath to go deeper. Breathe in . . . and out . . . Now breathe normally, easily, and effortlessly. Peace, peace, be still. Be still and be at peace. Let go, let go, let go, let go. Let go, let go, let God.

As you go deep within your being, let go of all cares and concerns of the day. Let yourself be quiet and still, and become one with Spirit. Merge into the utter quietude of your being. You are filled with peace and harmony. You are settled down to a state of deep rest and relaxation.

Now imagine you are seeing the entire planet from the viewpoint of outer space. The earth is a beautiful, deep-blue jewel, with sapphire oceans, landmasses of bright green forests, olive green plains, golden and sienna deserts, ornamented by white swirling clouds. The planet seems infinitesimally small and vulnerable compared to the vast outer space around it.

Seeing this view of our planet as a precious jewel, you now wonder how people can live in conflict. You are struck by the senseless, meaningless insanity of conflict, war, murder, intolerance, greed, bigotry, and cruelty that keep the world in chains of ignorance. The suffering of humanity weighs upon your heart.

Now notice within your heart a small divine flame igniting—the flame of unconditional love, fanned by the current of compassion for humanity. That flame begins to swell into a radiant love light that grows and expands in brilliance. Shining with pure crystalline clarity, that light begins to saturate and surround your being.

Now you are immersed in this pure love light, which fills your heart with fullness, joy, and contentment. Divine love now engulfs you in its purity and beauty. You are permeated, saturated, and surrounded with pure love, within and all around you.

This love is so powerful and magnificent that it begins to overflow. There is so much love within you that you cannot contain it. You ache to share it now with all of humanity, and it is now spilling over. Your heart begins to shine like a sun radiating light, as this beauteous love vibration emanates from within you.

The love within you now spreads outward and begins to fill up not only your energy field, but also the space around you. Soon it fills the entire room . . . It then becomes larger and expands to encompass the entire land around the building where you are . . .

Then this pure love, which is perpetually replenished in your heart, now vibrates and radiates outward into your town or city, permeating and surrounding it . . . This divine love then grows larger and more powerful as it fills your entire province or state . . .

Visualize this pure divine love now filling your entire nation . . . All the people of the nation are feeling soothed and comforted by this divine love. Then notice this powerful love vibration beginning to expand to other nations. As it spreads, it travels over the oceans to other continents. It spreads to North America . . . South America . . . Europe . . . Africa . . . Asia . . . Australia . . . and Oceana . . . Finally it encompasses the entire planet . . .

Divine love, radiating from your heart, now fills and surrounds the earth with its magnificence and glory. All of humanity is loved, nurtured, healed, and lifted by this pure love, which is now blanketing the entire planet . . .

As your heart expands to welcome, accept, and enfold all of humanity into its chamber of pure love, the entire world celebrates the dawn of a new age. It is an age of heaven on earth, where human beings no longer wage war. Peace on earth is declared now, and all the people live in harmony. All peoples of the earth of all races, who speak all languages, now extend their hands and reach out to each other.

Visualize them now, holding hands, encircling the entire earth, and dancing in great celebration and joy. All are singing a song, "Peace and harmony on earth, and brotherhood and sisterhood to all peoples." Take a few moments now to radiate pure divine love to touch the heart of every person on this planet. Take a couple of deep breaths and then remain in silence as you imagine spreading divine love throughout the world . . . [Record one minute of silence here.]

Now, with gratitude in your heart, keep your eyes closed as you come forth from the meditation by taking at least four deep vigorous breaths and pretend you are blowing out four candles . . . [Record fifteen seconds of silence here.] Then, come all the way back to objective and subjective balance and open your eyes . . .

Now speak the following affirmation audibly with your eyes wide open:

I AM alert . . . I AM awake . . . I AM very alert . . . I AM very awake . . . I AM objectively and subjectively balanced . . . I AM in control . . . I AM the only authority in my life . . . I AM divinely protected by the light of my being . . . Thank you, Spirit, and SO IT IS.

AFFIRMATION OF UNIVERSAL ACCEPTANCE

Say the following affirmation audibly in a clear voice with conviction:

This is an affirmation of universal acceptance for and with all humanity. I now know and recognize that there is one power and one presence in the universe and in my life, the divine Spirit. This power is the source of all good and the source of unconditional love, compassion, tolerance, and acceptance. Spirit accepts and welcomes all as its own with infinite forbearance, open-mindedness, kindness, permissiveness, leniency, and nonjudgment. Nothing is proprietary or excluded in Spirit.

I AM one with this divine power and presence in a perfect seamless wholeness, in total unity. I AM one with Spirit. I AM filled with tolerance, acceptance, forbearance, open-mindedness, kindness, permissiveness, leniency, and nonjudgment. I AM an infinite well of compassion and unconditional love.

I therefore now know and claim for and with all of humanity that all peoples of this earth are filled with universal acceptance, kindness, and unconditional brotherly and sisterly love, or better, now.

All negative feelings throughout this earth that no longer serve its inhabitants are now released from our minds. All feelings of intolerance, prejudice, hatred, bigotry, condemnation,

closed-mindedness, strictness, meanness, fanaticism, racism,
narrow-mindedness, sexism, chauvinism, extremism, zealotry,
partisanship, sanctimoniousness, inequity, and insularity are now
lifted, healed, released, dissolved, and completely let go into the
light of divine love and truth. They are burnt in the fire of divine
love, and they are gone.

All the peoples of earth now welcome and accept into
their minds, hearts, and emotions new, powerful, positive,
optimistic thoughts and emotions of acceptance, unconditional
love, tolerance, impartiality, broad-mindedness, patience,
kindness, leniency, permissiveness, evenhandedness, justice,
neutrality, objectivity, benevolence, altruism, humanity,
magnanimity, compassion, mercy, understanding, goodwill,
mildness, and tenderness.

This planet is a celebration of diversity and a melting pot of all
races, religions, ideologies, faiths, beliefs, and ways of living.
It is a glorious rainbow of varied cultures and traditions, all in
harmony and unconditional love. Despite their differences, all the
inhabitants on earth now live in harmonious accord, in tolerance,
compassion, and brotherly, and sisterly love.

I now accept fully and completely in consciousness all that I have
spoken, or better. I now release this affirmation fully and completely

into the Spiritual Law, knowing that it does manifest now, under divine grace, in Spirit's wise and perfect ways. And I thank Spirit that this is so now, and SO IT IS.

Make notes in your journal to describe what you experienced from practicing the affirmation and meditation in this chapter. In the next chapter, we'll open the doorway to ecological balance and sustainability of life on this planet.

Chapter 13

Open the Doorway to Ecological Balance

This chapter can help reverse the course of our planet, which is sliding quickly into ecological disasters of mega-proportions. By practicing the meditations and affirmations here, and by contributing to planetary balance through financial support and volunteerism, you can do your part to stop the madness of current policies and practices that are edging us ever closer to global un-sustainability.

AGRICULTURE AS NATURE INTENDED

Please record the following visualization on your device:

If you are listening to this as a recording, please close your eyes now and keep them closed throughout the visualization, until I tell you to open them.

Peace, peace, be still. Be still and be at peace. Peace, peace, be at peace. Be still and be at peace. Take a deep breath of divine love. Breathe in . . . and out . . . Take a deep breath of divine light. Breathe in . . . and out . . . Take a deep breath of forgiveness. Breathe in . . . and out . . . Take a big deep breath to go deeper. Breathe in . . . and out . . . Now relax and breathe normally.

We now call upon Gaia, Mother Earth, to assist in this visualization. Imagine this planet is now a garden in paradise. There is an abundance of healthy, nutritious food. All people on earth are fully nourished by healthy food brimming with nutrients, which is grown and raised with sustainable practices as intended by nature. Inhabitants of this planet are healthy, happy, and long-lived because their food is their medicine. They are no longer dependent upon pharmaceuticals. They are sustained by fresh organic food, pure water, and spiritual energy.

Imagine that sustainable agricultural practices are now restored to the earth. Farmers now grow a mixture of crops in the same area and practice multiyear crop rotations. Cover crops are planted in off-seasons. Tillage is eliminated, and integrated pest management is embraced without chemicals. Crops, trees, and animal production are all integrated in the same farms. Riparian buffers or prairie strips are restored. Pollinators such as bees and other biodiverse species are sustained in healthy populations.

Imagine the sea life is no longer plundered by unsustainable fishing practices. The oceans are no longer used as trash dumps. They are now cleansed, cleared, and cleaned of all toxic materials that are harmful to sea creatures. The world's coral reefs are now restored. All the freshwater and seawater sources on this planet are cleansed and cleared of pollutants. All the fresh water is now potable, because humans no longer use their precious water sources to dump their waste.

Imagine solar, wind, and hydroelectric are the main power sources on the planet. Coal is no longer mined and burned, petroleum is no longer pumped to the surface, and nuclear power is now defunct. Trees are planted to absorb carbon emissions. Forests are restored and their land is not used for agriculture or building materials. The atmosphere of the planet is now in balance. The ozone layer is restored.

Mother Gaia now celebrates victory and expresses gratitude to the unsung heroes and heroines who work persistently and tirelessly to restore the planet. Now take a few moments of silence to visualize the earth as a paradise, and humanity now enjoying robust health, well-being, and longevity. See all living creatures on the planet now living in health and harmony . . . [Record fifteen seconds of silence here.]

Then, with gratitude in your heart, keep your eyes closed as you come forth from the meditation by taking at least four deep vigorous breaths and pretend you are blowing out four candles . . . [Record fifteen seconds of silence here.] Then, come all the way back to objective and subjective balance and open your eyes . . .

Now repeat the following affirmation audibly with your eyes open:

I AM alert . . . I AM awake . . . I AM very alert . . . I AM very awake . . . I AM objectively and subjectively balanced . . . I AM in control . . . I AM the only authority in my life . . . I AM divinely protected by the light of my being . . . Thank you, Spirit, and SO IT IS.

ECOLOGICAL AWARENESS

Please say this affirmation audibly in a clear, confident, and convincing voice:

The world is as I AM. The health and well-being of this planet are my own responsibility. I AM a keeper and maintainer of ecological balance on earth.

My every thought, word, and deed profoundly affect this planet. My attitude, intentions, and beliefs influence all life on earth. I AM the world and the world is what I AM. The earth is my home, and I now treat it with honor and respect. I see, know, and accept that I now take steps to heal the planet.

Everything I do now supports the healing of this planet.
My pocketbook now sponsors sustainable living.
I now support sustainable food production practices.
I now support planetary diversity.
I now support a planet that sustains life.
I now support a planet with clean food, clean water, and clean air.
My world is a paradise, and I live in it conscientiously.
Thank you, Spirit, and SO BE IT.

NATURAL HEALING—FREE FROM POISON

It is my experience that natural healing practices can be highly effective, and many diseases can be overcome without ingesting poisonous chemicals. However, the affirmation below should not be construed as medical advice.

Please speak this affirmation audibly in a confident and convincing voice:

I recognize that there is one healing presence at work in the
universe and in my life, the divine Spirit. That healing presence has
created innate healing power in all living beings, as well as natural
substances on this planet that bring restoration and renewal. Spirit
is the one renewer and restorer of health and well-being. It heals all
and makes all things new. Spirit is perfect health and wholeness.

I AM one with, merged with, and the same as Spirit, which fills and surrounds me now with perfect health and well-being. I AM wholeness and oneness, now and always. I AM now one with the innate healing power of my body to restore and renew itself, and I AM now one with the natural healing properties of substances provided by nature.

I therefore know and claim that I AM healed now in natural ways, without polluting my body or the atmosphere with poisonous substances. I AM now willing to consider using natural remedies, treatments, and therapies that restore life and do not exacerbate illness. I now support preventative medicine and other ethical natural-healing practices.

I now trust my intuition regarding health decisions, and I ask pertinent questions to physicians who are advising me. I now make health decisions based not only upon advice from competent health professionals, but also upon investigative research, inner wisdom, and common sense. I let go of dependency upon poisonous pharmaceuticals that may be addictive or may bring devastating side effects. I now find additional or alternative ways to bring healing and well-being to my body.

I now accept fully in consciousness all that I have spoken, or better, and I give gratitude to Spirit for my perfect robust health and well-being. I now release this affirmation into the Spiritual Law, and I thank Spirit that this manifests now in my life. I give gratitude that this is so now, and SO IT IS.

Take a moment to make a note in your journal to describe what you experienced from practicing the meditation and affirmations in this chapter. In the next chapter, you'll open the doorway to world peace.

Chapter 14

Open the Doorway to World Peace

My spiritual mentor Maharishi Mahesh Yogi often used to say, "For the forest to be green, all the trees must be green. For the world to be at peace, all the individuals must be at peace." I agree with this grassroots approach. Perhaps the best way to achieve world peace is for the population to become more peaceful through meditation and other spiritual practices. Thereby we'll radiate peacefulness to the environment and contribute to world peace.

LET THERE BE PEACE ON EARTH BEGINNING WITH ME

Please speak this affirmation audibly in a confident and clear voice:

Let there be peace on earth, and let it begin with me.
I AM the peacemaker, and I radiate harmonious thoughts.
I AM the peacemaker, and I speak wise words.
I AM the peacemaker, and I perform meritorious deeds.

I contribute to world peace
Through all that I think, all that I say, and all that I do.
I AM peace, I think peace, I speak peace, and I do peace.

I AM peace. I AM love. I AM harmony.
I AM peace. I AM love. I AM harmony.
I AM peace. I AM love. I AM harmony.

Peace is the lighthouse of my life.
Peace is my way-shower.
I AM the peace messenger.

I AM the peacemaker. I AM at peace.
Thank you, Spirit, and SO IT IS.

WORLD PEACE VISUALIZATION

Please record the following meditation on your device:

If you are listening to this as a recording, please close your eyes now and keep them closed throughout the meditation, until I tell you to open them.

Peace, peace, be still. Be still and be at peace. Peace, peace, be at peace. Be still and be at peace. Perfect peace, perfect peace, perfect peace. Be still and be at peace. Take a deep breath of divine love. Breathe in . . . and out . . . Take a deep breath of divine light. Breathe in . . . and out . . . Take a deep breath of relaxation. Breathe in . . . and out . . . Now relax and breathe normally. Let go, let go, let go, let go. Let go, let go, let God.

We now know and recognize that there is one power and one presence in the universe and in our lives—the divine Spirit. Spirit is the source of world peace and global harmony. Spirit is tranquility, serenity, stillness, oneness, and wholeness.

We are now one with Spirit. We are merged with Spirit in a perfect seamless wholeness. There is no separation between Spirit and us. We are perfectly allied and aligned with Spirit right here and now. Therefore we are the source of world peace and global harmony. We are tranquility, serenity, stillness, oneness, and wholeness.

We therefore now know and claim that the world is at peace. The entire earth now lives in harmony, unconditional love, acceptance, kindness, unity, and celebration.

We now release from the minds of all peoples on earth all negative thoughts, feelings, and emotions that have caused conflicts and wars. The people of earth now release fear, greed, war, intolerance, fanaticism, zealotry, inhumanity, cruelty, genocide, oppression, domination, coercion, dictatorship, ignorance, terrorism, dogmatism, conquest, cult leadership, and enforced religious conversion. These thoughts are now lifted, healed, released, dissolved, and let go from the minds and hearts of all people on this planet now. And they are gone. They are lifted into the light of divine truth.

The people on this planet now welcome into their hearts and minds new creative thoughts of faith, trust, generosity, peace, tolerance, forbearance, acceptance, patience, kindness, humanitarianism, benevolence, human rights, elective government, equality, rule of law, freedom of thought, freedom of speech, freedom of assembly, and freedom of religion. The people of earth now live in peace and harmony.

Now visualize all nations of the world coming together in world peace amidst diversity. All nations and religions enjoy freedom to govern and worship in their own unique ways, and there is harmony, humanity, tolerance, compassion, and love amongst all people.

Envision all the nations working together in harmonious pluralism, creating sustainable agriculture, curing disease, wiping out poverty, creating prosperity, supporting scientific progress, educating all children, creating employment for all, eradicating drug addiction, eliminating crime, healing mental illness, supporting artistic endeavors, and spreading worldwide happiness, peace, love, and compassion.

Imagine our green planet is now a paradise. All its inhabitants enjoy personal integrity—free from blame, resentment, persecution, victim mind-set, and irresponsibility. All do their part to contribute to a world of peace and progress.

Now contemplate what you can do to make the world a better place. How can you advance civilization to a higher level of awareness?

Spend a few moments considering what you can do *now* to contribute to world peace . . . [Record one minute of silence here.]

Now, with gratitude in your heart, keep your eyes closed as you come forth from the visualization by taking at least four deep vigorous breaths and pretend you are blowing out four candles . . . [Record fifteen seconds of silence here.] Then, come all the way back to objective and subjective balance and open your eyes . . .

Now repeat the following affirmation audibly with your eyes open: *I AM alert . . . I AM awake . . . I AM very alert . . . I AM very awake . . . I AM objectively and subjectively balanced . . . I AM in control . . . I AM the only authority in my life . . . I AM divinely protected by the light of my being . . . Thank you, Spirit, and SO IT IS.*

VISUALIZING HEAVEN ON EARTH

This will be a "writing meditation." Please get out a piece of paper and a pen and get ready to write.

Imagine a world at peace where all people on the planet live in harmony and happiness. On your piece of paper, please write a description of this earth if there were no war, no crime, no avarice, no bigotry, and no violence. What would the earth be like? Please write descriptions of the following categories:

1. What families would be like.

2. What the educational system would be like.

3. What personal relationships would be like.

4. What towns and cities would be like.

5. How the budget for government agencies would be funded and allocated.

6. What the workplace would be like.

7. What nations would be like.

8. What political leaders would be like.

9. What the health care system would be like.

10. What professions would be valued and paid the most.

11. What the most profitable businesses would be.

12. What projects the entertainment industry would create.

13. Any other details you care to envision.

After you've written this paper, ask yourself if there is a way to make one change in your life that will take this planet one step closer to heaven on earth. Can you speak more kindly to strangers? Can you be more empathetic to your employees? Can you make your spouse's day more cheerful? How can you contribute towards world peace in your life today?

After all, who is creating heaven on earth or hell on earth? Who is creating conflict or world peace? It's every individual who walks the earth.

Now write in your journal and describe what you experienced when you practiced the affirmation, meditation, and exercise in this chapter. In the next chapter, you'll begin to illuminate spiritual enlightenment as you open the doorway to intuition and inner wisdom.

Part IV

Illuminating Spiritual Enlightenment

Chapter 15

Open the Doorway to Intuition and Wisdom

My Divine Revelation® guided meditation can help you receive divine guidance, love, healing, wisdom, and inspiration from within. The premise of the method is this: "Ask, and it shall be given unto you."

I have written several books about this powerful meditation technique, including *Divine Revelation* and *Awaken Your Divine Intuition*. In those books I delve deeply into how to practice and use it. Please consider the meditation here as a brief introduction to an entire wealth of information you can learn about this method in detail, step-by-step, by studying these other books.

DIVINE REVELATION GUIDED MEDITATION

Please prepare for the meditation by making a recording on your device. Go to page 140, line 6, and record the meditation script. Then, when you are ready to practice it, first verbalize the following affirmations audibly with certainty, strength, and conviction. Then play back the recording.

I now recognize that there is one power and one presence at work in the universe and in my life, the divine presence. I am one with the power, light, love, peace, joy, and purity of this perfect presence now. I am one with the truth of my being, with the light of Spirit— one with wholeness, oneness, and wisdom.

I therefore claim the perfect experience of the Divine Revelation meditation now that proceeds perfectly with divine order and timing. I now know that during this meditation I receive spiritual awakening as much as I can comfortably enjoy. I receive direct divine contact and communication, and clear, precise messages from Spirit. I receive divine love and healing. I experience the profound reality of absolute bliss consciousness within. I receive all that is highest wisdom for me to receive in this meditation—all this and better. Thank you, Spirit, and SO IT IS.

I AM in control. I AM the only authority in my life. I AM divinely protected by the light of my being. I close off my aura and body of light to the lower astral levels of mind. And I open to the spiritual world.

I invoke the divine presence to help me eliminate negations and limitations that prevent me from a deep meditation experience. I now dispel all feelings of tension, stress, anxiety, fear, frustration, resentment, anger, guilt, blame, sadness, pain, and all other thoughts and emotions that do not reflect the truth of my being. Instead I now welcome feelings of relaxation, peace, trust, faith, confidence, effortlessness, ease, forgiveness, letting go, compassion, happiness, and comfort. I AM in control. I thank Spirit, AND SO IT IS.

I now heal and lift any interfering entities and energies from the astral plane that might be blocking this process of meditation. Beloved ones, you are unified with the truth of your being. You are lifted in divine love and forgiven of all guilt and shame. You are healed, loosed, and released from loss, pain, confusion, and fear. Divine love and divine light fill and surround you now. Attachment to the earth no longer binds you. You are free to go into the divine light now, dear ones. Go now in peace and love.

I call upon Spirit to cut any and all psychic ties, cords, connections, karmic bonds, and binding ties between myself and any person, place, thing, organization, situation, circumstance, memory, experience, or addiction that prevents my experience of deep meditation. These psychic bonds are now lovingly cut, cut,

cut, cut, cut, cut, cut, cut, cut, cut, cut, cut, cut, cut, cut, lifted, loved, healed, released, and let go, into the light of divine love and truth. Thank you Spirit, AND SO IT IS.

Please record the following meditation on your device, and play it back after speaking the previous affirmations audibly:

If you are listening to this as a recording, please close your eyes now and keep them closed throughout the meditation, until I tell you to open them.

Peace, peace, be still. Be still and be at peace. Peace, peace, be at peace. Be still and be at peace. Perfect peace, perfect peace, perfect peace. Be still and be at peace. Take a deep breath of divine love. Breathe in . . . and out . . . Take a deep breath of divine light. Breathe in . . . and out . . . Take a deep breath of relaxation. Breathe in . . . and out . . . Take a big deep breath to go deeper. Breathe in . . . and out . . . Deeper, deeper, deeper into the wells of Spirit, into the silence of being. Breathe in . . . and out . . . Now relax, relax, release, and be at peace. Relax, relax, release, and be at peace. Breathe normally, easily, and effortlessly. Let go, let go, let go, let go. Let go, let go, let God.

Now relax your mind and let go of the environment . . . Any sounds around you only serve to take you deeper into meditation. Release and let go of all cares and concerns. Whatever limiting thoughts or negative beliefs you have brought here, now hand them over to Spirit. Release and let go of these limitations now as you take a big deep breath to go deeper. Breathe in . . . and out . . . Now breathe normally.

Now become aware of your physical body . . . Anywhere you feel any sensation, tension, or stress, just allow your attention and awareness to simply rest on that place or places within the body that are drawing your attention. As you place attention on those sensations, take a few moments of quietude to allow them to dissipate . . . [Record fifteen seconds of silence here.] Now take a deep breath. Breathe in . . . and out . . . Then breathe normally to go deeper, deeper, into the wells of Spirit.

Now become aware that the physical body is becoming very relaxed, quiet, and still. The breath rate is becoming quieter and subtler. The heart rate and blood pressure are settling down to deep relaxation. The body is filled with health and well-being. Take a big deep breath now. Breathe in . . . and out . . . Take another deep breath to fill the entire body with deep relaxation and peace. Breathe in . . . and out . . . Now breathe normally. Relax, relax, release. Completely let go and give up. Relax, relax, release, and go deeper. Peace, peace, be still. Be still and be at peace.

Now become aware of the conscious mind. As the body settles to deep relaxation, the conscious mind now settles down to complete quietude. As the breathing becomes subtler, and the body becomes relaxed, the mind becomes quiet and serene. So tranquil and relaxed, like a still pond, without a ripple. Take a big deep breath to go even deeper into the silence. Breathe in . . . and out . . . Then breathe normally. Peace, peace, be still. Be still and be at peace.

Now allow the attention to drift into the subconscious realm. As you move through the subconscious, your mind settles down to even deeper peace and relaxation. It rests in deep silence and peace, like the water at the bottom of the ocean, submerged in total stillness, calm, and serenity, at the depth of that silent ocean. Now take a big deep breath and go deeper, deeper, into the wells of Spirit. Breathe in . . . and out . . . Then breathe normally. Peace, peace, be still. Relax, release, and be at peace.

Now take another big deep breath. Breathe in . . . and out . . . Then breathe normally. Now become aware of a seeming veil that has separated you from Spirit and has caused you to identify yourself as your false ego. Now penetrate that veil and walk through it quietly and effortlessly. Then cross over the rainbow bridge that leads into the realm of Spirit.

Now open your heart to Spirit and welcome the divine presence in love. Bathe in the radiant light of Spirit, where you are now cleansed and healed. Magnificent streams of heavenly energy now flood into your being, vibrating and radiating around you. Now absorb the light of the sacred, eternal oneness of Spirit. You are filled with exaltation and inspiration. Now take another big deep breath and go deeper.

Breathe in . . . and out . . . Then breathe normally. Deeper, deeper, deeper, into the wells of Spirit, into the silence of being. Relax, release, and be at peace. Peace, peace, be still.

Now become aware of your etheric soul self, your immortal, eternal soul, which is effulgent, beauteous, radiant, filled with splendor, ever youthful, joyous, and imperishable. Now take a moment to consciously ask your soul self to come forth now and introduce itself to you . . . Then take a few moments to ask this luminous being to reveal your soul's purpose and true desires to you . . . [Record one minute of silence here.]

Now take a deep breath and go even deeper. Breathe in . . . and out . . . Then breathe normally. Deeper, deeper, into relaxation and silence . . . Now go to the level of your Christ self. Take a moment to ask this brilliant being of golden light to reveal itself to you, that you may recognize the unconditional love, healing, compassion, and redemption of your inner Christ self . . . [Record fifteen seconds of silence here.]

Now take another deep breath. Breathe in . . . and out . . . Then breathe normally. Now go deeper into the silence of being, as you call upon your "I AM" self to come forth and reveal its splendiferous light of wisdom, beingness, awareness, and consciousness. This beautiful, powerful, mighty "I AM" presence is now present in all its glory . . .

Take another deep breath, Breathe in . . . and out . . . Then breathe normally. Go deeper, deeper, into the silence of being . . . Now become aware of the God self, with humility, devotion and love. Approach your higher self at the altar of inner divinity. God is right here within you, at the center of your being, now and always—omnipotent, omnipresent, omniscient, radiant, and filled with luminosity . . .

Now take another deep breath. Breathe in . . . and out . . . Then breathe normally. Let go and let Spirit take you deeper, deeper still, into the wells of Spirit, into the silence of being . . . Relax and let go into the cosmic self, vast and immense as the entire universe. All the stars, galaxies, and planets, the enormous reaches of the universe are contained within your cosmic self, without limits. . .

Now take a deep breath and go deeper. Breathe in . . . and out . . . Then breathe normally. As you relax and let go, your attention sinks even deeper, deeper still, into the center of being, into the wells of inner silence. Take a deep breath now. Breathe in . . . and out . . . Then breathe normally.

Now let go and allow your awareness to settle down to the perfection of your being. Beyond the realm of duality, now transcend into the nameless, formless, quality-less, motionless absolute. Take a deep breath now. Breathe in . . . and out . . . Then breathe normally. Now ask the divine presence to take you deeper, into unbounded awareness at the center of being. Then take a few moments to dwell in that deep silence. If, at any time, you feel you are getting out of the silence, take a deep breath to go back in . . . [Record one minute of silence here.]

Peace, peace, be still. Be still and be at peace. Perfect peace, perfect peace, perfect peace. Be still, and be at peace.

Now say the following affirmation audibly:

I now call upon the divine presence . . . my higher self . . . to come forth now . . . and bring me a message . . . of highest wisdom for today . . . Please give me a message . . . that will deepen my inner contact . . . with the divine . . . uplift me, heal me . . . and bring forth divine inspiration . . . wisdom, and joy . . .

Now relax and let go. Get quiet and still, and practice the do-nothing program: Do nothing, nothing, and less than nothing. Have a neutral attitude, yet be willing to receive. Ask your higher self to speak to you. You'll receive the message as a vision, a voice, or a feeling. These are the three main ways Spirit speaks to you.

You might get a clairvoyant vision, like a motion picture in your inner eye. Or you may get a clairsentient feeling or a sensing of truth. Or you may hear inspiring clairaudient words in your mind or heart. This will sound like any other thought passing through your mind. But these loving, wise words will speak from a deeper source, from the presence of Spirit.

Now repeat after me the following words audibly:

"Holy Spirit, please give me your message . . . or answer the question . . . that is in my heart, now . . . "

Now take three big deep breaths, and go deep within, into the silence of your being, and do the do-nothing program. Do nothing, nothing, and less than nothing. Maintain a neutral attitude, without expectations, yet be open and willing to receive the message. If at any time during the silence you lose contact with Spirit, just take a deep breath and ask Spirit to take you deeper. Then let go and do nothing . . .[Record four minutes of silence here.]

Peace, peace, be still. Be still and be at peace. Perfect peace, perfect peace, perfect peace. Be still and be at peace.

Now it's time to give gratitude and come out of meditation. Please keep your eyes closed until I tell you to open them. Give gratitude to Spirit for this wonderful meditation and for all you have received today.

Then take a big deep breath and pretend you are blowing out a candle . . . Come forth now and know that the subconscious mind has been permanently transformed and lifted by this meditation. The subconscious is now healed of false, limited beliefs, habits, and conditioning, as you let go and place the subconscious mind into the hands of Spirit.

Now take another deep breath and blow out another candle . . . Know that your conscious mind is now one with Spirit, one with the truth of your being. It is now united with divine mind. Every thought is a divine revelation and inspiration from Spirit.

Take another big deep breath and blow out a third candle . . . Now know that your body has been transformed and lifted by this meditation. Your physical body is one with the divine body and is transmuted into a radiant body of pure light, brilliance, and splendor, in perfect robust health.

Take another big deep breath and blow out a fourth candle as you notice the environment, yet still keeping your eyes closed. Notice your body sitting in the chair, the space around you, coming back to this time and place. You now bring into the environment all you have gained from this meditation—all the gifts of Spirit.

You are a glowing being of light and messenger of Spirit, vibrating and beaming the divine presence all around you in every precious moment. You are a walking, talking, breathing, living vessel of Spirit, and you recognize the magnificence of your being. You now let go and allow Spirit to guide you daily.

Now take four deep vigorous breaths and blow out four candles . . . [Record fifteen seconds of silence here.] Then come all the way back to inward and outward balance and open your eyes . . . With your eyes open, verbalize the following affirmation audibly in a powerful voice, with clarity and conviction:

I AM alert . . . I AM awake . . . I AM very alert . . . I AM very awake . . . I AM inwardly and outwardly balanced . . . I AM in control . . . I AM the only authority in my life . . . I AM divinely protected by the light of my being . . . Thank you, Spirit, and SO IT IS . . .

In your journal, write a description of what you experienced practicing the meditation in this chapter. To learn more about how to receive, evaluate, test, trust, and follow your divine intuition safely by using specific signals and a field-proven ten-test system, please study these two books: *Divine Revelation* and *Awaken Your Divine Intuition.* In the next chapter, you'll open the doorway to wholeness and oneness.

Chapter 16

Open the Doorway to Wholeness and Oneness

At the center of your being is perfect completeness and contentment. Your higher self is the truth of your being. When you realize your true nature, you will discover you are an infinite sphere whose center is everywhere and whose circumference is nowhere.

UNBOUNDED AWARENESS MEDITATION

Please record the following meditation onto your device:

If you are listening to this as a recording, please close your eyes now and keep them closed throughout the meditation, until I tell you to open them.

Peace, peace, be still. Be still and be at peace. Peace, peace, be at peace. Be still and be at peace. Perfect peace, perfect peace, perfect peace. Be still and be at peace. Take a deep breath of divine love.

Breathe in . . . and out . . . Take a deep breath of divine light. Breathe in . . . and out . . . Take a deep breath of relaxation. Breathe in . . . and out . . . Now relax and breathe normally. Let go, let go, let go, let go. Let go, let go, let God.

Take a big deep breath to go deeper. Breathe in . . . and out . . . Now breathe normally, easily, and effortlessly. Deeper, deeper, deeper into the wells of Spirit, into the silence of being. Relax, relax, release. Release and be at peace.

Imagine you are floating on a pond that is warm, still, and silent. There is no ripple on the pond, and the sun is shining, reflecting on the water, which is mirroring perfectly the sky, the clouds, and the trees. There is a soft, warm breeze. It is so quiet and serene. No feeling is there other than tranquility. No sound is there other than an occasional song of a lark. You have never felt more at peace.

As you immerse yourself in that placid pool of peace, you are cleansed of all seeming negative energies. In that pond, you are washed clean in the waters of pure love and contentment. You feel you could float in that pond forever and enjoy the comfort of its warm healing waters.

You feel completely refreshed as you step out of the pond and give gratitude to its healing waters. You are dry, warm, and comfortable, and you are now wearing fresh white linen garments. Begin to walk into a green meadow, studded with fragrant wildflowers and capped by an azure sky, a bright sun, and wind-swept clouds that form the shape of winged angels.

You have picked the perfect spot to meditate under a wide oak shade tree. The temperature is warm, and you feel completely relaxed. A comfortable chair appears under the tree branches, and you sit down and close your eyes.

As you move deep within, into the silence, imagine a beauteous light enters into your body from above. It is the divine light, the light of Spirit. That light fills you with radiance and peace. That pure light begins to grow as you imagine it expanding to permeate, pervade, fill, and surround you. The light is glowing and radiating as your awareness begins to expand.

Now envision your awareness growing larger and larger. Your conscious awareness is expanding beyond the boundaries of your body. It is reaching outward beyond this meadow, this tree, and into the sky, beyond the earth, beyond the atmosphere, beyond the stratosphere, and into outer space.

As you move into the void of outer space, you are no longer bound to your body. You are beyond your mind. You have left behind the limitations of your ego. Your awareness is expanding far beyond this world and into the farthest reaches of the universe.

As your consciousness expands, it fills the entire universe. And as you become as limitless as the universe, you embody a cosmic self that is as large and vast as the entire cosmos, and everything in the universe is within your cosmic body. The void of empty space, all the stars and galaxies, and all the inhabitants in the universe are within your cosmic body.

As your awareness grows even larger, you transcend all boundaries, and become measureless and incalculable. There are no limitations. You are the cosmos and you embody it. You touch the infinite, beyond time, space, and causation, for the universe is your very soul essence. There is no separation between you and everything in this universe. Therefore, you are one with, the same as, and unified with all. There is no sense of another, for you are only one, and there is no second. You dwell in a perfect seamless oneness, beyond all differences.

Now take a few moments to enjoy the endless universe and the timeless absolute in deep silence . . . [Record thirty seconds of silence here.]

Peace, peace, be still. Be still and be at peace. Perfect peace, perfect peace, perfect peace. Be still, and be at peace. Now place your attention on your physical body, and sense what your body feels like . . . [Record 15 minutes of silence here.]

Now give gratitude to Spirit for this wonderful meditation and for all you have received today, and come out of meditation step by step. Please keep your eyes closed until I tell you to open them.

Take a big deep breath and pretend you are blowing out a candle . . . Come forth now and become aware of your subconscious mind. Then blow out another candle . . . Become aware of your conscious mind. Now blow out a third candle . . . Become aware of your physical body . . . Your mind and body have been permanently lifted and transformed by this meditation. Then blow out another candle as you become aware of the environment, yet still keeping your eyes closed . . . Become aware of your body sitting in the chair, the space around you, coming back to this time and place. You are now bringing into your life all the expansion of awareness you have gained from this meditation.

Now take four deep vigorous breaths and blow out four candles . . . [Record fifteen seconds of silence here.] Then come all the way back to inward and outward balance and then open your eyes . . .

With eyes open, speak the following affirmation audibly in a powerful voice with clarity and conviction:

I AM alert . . . I AM awake . . . I AM very alert . . . I AM very awake . . . I AM inwardly and outwardly balanced . . . I AM in control . . . I AM the only authority in my life . . . I AM divinely protected by the light of my being . . . Thank you, Spirit, and SO IT IS.

ONENESS AFFIRMATION

Say this affirmation audibly in a clear voice with conviction and feeling:

I AM oneness. I AM wholeness.

I AM one with my divine nature, my true self.

I AM filled and surrounded with divine love and light.

I AM one with Spirit. I AM one with the infinite.

I AM one with my inner divinity.

I AM whole, complete, and perfect in every way.

No one and nothing can adversely affect my true divine nature.

I AM invincible, indestructible, and unassailable.

I AM mighty, strong, powerful, and at peace.

Thank you, Spirit, and SO IT IS.

ONENESS MANTRA

Below is a traditional mantra that can help you experience oneness and wholeness as your true nature of being. It's called the "Savitri Gayatri Mantra," and millions of people worldwide chant it daily. It's a prayer to *Savitri*, the Solar Orb, found in the scripture *Rig-Veda*, III.62.10. I strongly recommend you learn how to pronounce it by listening to it online. Search the Shemaroo Bhakti channel on YouTube for "Gayatri Mantra—Meaning & Significance."

Please speak the mantra audibly in a clear voice:

OM Bhur Bhuvah Swaha.

Tat Savitur Varenyam.

Bhargo Devasya Dheemahi.

Dhiyo Yonah Prachodayaat.

Here's a translation of the mantra:

"I meditate on that most adored Supreme Lord, the creator, like the sun, the source of all life, whose effulgence illumines all realms (physical, mental, and spiritual). May this divine light illumine my intellect."

Chanting or meditating with this mantra invokes divine light to lift your energy field. This mantra has untold benefits, including acting in highest wisdom, speaking with sweetness, clarity of mind, greater discernment, following your true purpose, fulfilling your destiny, and attaining enlightenment.

Please describe in your journal what you experienced practicing the meditation and affirmations in this chapter. In the next chapter, you'll open the doorway to higher spiritual lifting.

Chapter 17

Open the Doorway to Spiritual Lifting

In this chapter you'll practice meditations and affirmations that can lift your awareness to higher consciousness so you can realize your true divine nature, which is absolute perfection and bliss.

SPIRITUAL LIFTING MEDITATION

Please record the following meditation onto your device:

If you are listening to this as a recording, please close your eyes now and keep them closed throughout the meditation, until I tell you to open them.

Peace, peace, be still. Be still and be at peace. Peace, peace, be at peace. Be still and be at peace. Perfect peace, perfect peace, perfect peace. Be still and be at peace. Take a deep breath of divine love.

Breathe in . . . and out . . . Take a deep breath of divine light. Breathe in . . . and out . . . Take a deep breath of relaxation. Breathe in . . . and out . . . Take a big deep breath to go deeper. Breathe in . . . and out . . . Now relax and breathe normally. Let go, let go, let go, let go, let go, let go, let God.

Breathe in . . . and out . . . Breathe normally and peacefully. Peace, peace, be still. Be still and be at peace. Perfect peace, perfect peace, perfect peace. Be still and be at peace. Relax, relax, release, and be at peace. Now open your heart to receive the light of Spirit. Open your heart to be lifted into divine love. Open to divine grace and blessings. Open to the divine presence. You are blessed and beloved and filled with divine love.

Now repeat verbally in an audible voice, "Spirit, please lift me into higher consciousness now" . . . Then take a big deep breath to go deeper. Breathe in . . . and out . . . Deeper, deeper, deeper into the wells of Spirit, into the silence of being. Now breathe normally. We call upon Spirit to fill and surround you with a pure light that lifts your vibration and lifts the atmosphere of the place where you are meditating now.

We call upon divine beings of light who come in the name of God to encircle you and fill you with divine love, light, peace, safety, and security. You now reside in the mystical circle of divine protection. You now dwell in the realm of Spirit.

Open to receive divine love and light that Spirit is feeding you now. Imagine your mind is now settling down to quieter and quieter levels of awareness . . . Your mind is now letting go of the outer world and becoming aware of finer and finer states of consciousness . . .

Become aware of your body and allow your breathing and heartbeat to become quiet and relaxed . . . Your mind is becoming still, tranquil, and serene, like a quiet pool of water without a ripple . . . Imagine your subconscious mind becoming peaceful and silent, like the water at the bottom of the ocean . . .

Now notice whatever seems to be separating you from Spirit. It might be a veil, a bridge, a door, a gate, or a brick wall. Breathe in . . . and out . . . Once again, breathe in . . . and out . . . And one more big deep breath. Breathe in . . . and out . . . Then breathe normally and peacefully.

Now visualize that you easily, effortlessly, and simply walk through that barrier into Spirit. Let yourself glide through the seeming barricade and then open your heart to Spirit. As you walk through the gateway, you are lifted, lifted, lifted, higher and higher, into the perfection of being. Spirit welcomes you with open arms, and you now joyfully embrace and celebrate this divine connection.

Allow yourself to merge and melt into Spirit and become one with that divine presence. You are now in perfect peace, dwelling in the heart of Spirit. You are deeply loved. You are not alone. And you will never be alone again.

Now there is no separation between yourself and Spirit. You are unified in a perfect seamless wholeness. Spirit and you are one. Now ask audibly, "Please lift me into absolute bliss consciousness" . . . Then take a big deep breath. Breathe in . . . and out . . . Once again, breathe in . . . and out . . . And one more big deep breath. Breathe in . . . and out . . . Then breathe normally and peacefully.

Lifting, lifting, lifting, into the light of divine love and peace. You are being lifted into the truth of your being. Waves of bliss now engulf you and overtake your awareness. You are relaxed, at peace, content, and centered, in a state of perfect balance and equanimity. You are perfection everywhere now. You are perfection here now.

Let go, let go, let go, let go. Let go, let go, let God. You are now lifting into the blessed state of absolute bliss consciousness, whole and complete. You are now free to be your true self. You are now fully merged, one with, and aligned with pure consciousness. You are home in the heart of pure bliss.

Now spend a few moments in this state of higher consciousness . . . [Record thirty seconds of silence here.]

Now give gratitude to Spirit for this wonderful meditation and come out of meditation step by step. Please keep your eyes closed until I tell you to open them.

Take a big deep breath and pretend you are blowing out a candle . . . Come forth now and become aware of your subconscious mind. Then blow out another candle . . . Become aware of your conscious mind. Now blow out another candle . . . Become aware of your physical body. Then blow out another candle as you become aware of the environment, yet still keeping your eyes closed . . .

Now, with eyes closed, take a few more deep vigorous breaths and blow out more candles . . . [Record fifteen seconds of silence here.] Then come all the way back to inward and outward balance and open your eyes . . .

With eyes open, speak the following affirmation audibly in a powerful voice:

I AM alert . . . I AM awake . . . I AM very alert . . . I AM very awake . . . I AM objectively and subjectively balanced . . . I AM in control . . . I AM the only authority in my life . . . I AM divinely protected by the light of my being . . . Thank you, Spirit, and SO IT IS.

REALIZING YOUR TRUE SELF

This affirmation of spiritual integration is adapted from an ancient poem by perhaps the greatest saint that ever lived in India: Adi Shankara. Say this affirmation audibly with a clear voice, with certainty:

I AM not the body. I AM not the mind.
I AM not the intellect. I AM not the ego.
I AM not the ears, the tongue,
Nor the senses of smell or sight.
I AM not ether, nor air.
I AM eternal bliss and awareness.

I AM Spirit.
I AM not the life force energy,
Nor the elements of the physical body,
Nor the subtle body,
Nor hands, nor feet,
Nor any other limb of the body.
I AM eternal bliss and awareness.
I AM Spirit.
I have no fear, greed, or delusion.
I have no loathing or liking.
I possess no pride or ego of dharma or liberation.
I have neither mental desire,
Nor do I seek any object of desire.
I AM eternal bliss and awareness.
I AM Spirit.
I know neither pleasure nor pain.
I know not virtue and vice,
Neither mantra nor sacred place.
I know not spiritual study or rituals.
I AM not the eater, the food, or the meal.
I AM eternal bliss and awareness.
I AM Spirit.
I have no fear or pain.

I have no distinction of class.
I have neither father nor mother.
I have no birth or death.
I have neither friend nor comrade.
I have neither disciple nor guru.
I AM eternal bliss and awareness.
I AM Spirit.
I have no name, form, or fancy.
I AM the all-pervading.
I exist everywhere,
Yet I AM beyond the senses.
I AM not salvation.
I AM nothing to be known.
I AM eternal bliss and awareness.
I AM Spirit.

CHAKRA VISUALIZATION

This visualization can help you awaken the energy centers (known as "chakras"), increase the life force flowing through your subtle body, and raise your consciousness.

Please record the following visualization on your device:

If you are listening to this as a recording, please close your eyes now and keep them closed throughout the meditation, until I tell you to open them.

Peace, peace, be still. Be still and be at peace. Peace, peace, be at peace. Be still and be at peace. Perfect peace, perfect peace, perfect peace. Be still and be at peace. Take a deep breath of divine love. Breathe in . . . and out . . . Take a deep breath of divine light. Breathe in . . . and out . . . Take a deep breath of relaxation. Breathe in . . . and out . . . Now relax and breathe normally.

Now place your attention at your tailbone, at the base of your spine. Imagine a lotus-shaped flower with four bright red petals continually spinning and radiating red rays. This is called the "root chakra," the energy center of primal life force and survival, responsible for bodily excretion. In its center is a luminous yellow square, embodying the earth element. It is surrounded by eight shining spears.

A brilliant triangle resides within the square. Within the triangle, a deep red energy, associated with sexual desire, shines like millions of suns. This energy vibrates a seed mantra: *kling*—the mantra of desire. Within the triangle resides a masculine power, a flawless void, the abode of all deities and powers. Everything gets absorbed into it, and it supports all. Luminous, imperishable, perfect, and omnipresent, it bestows bliss and all that is good. *Kundalini,* a spiral-shaped feminine power resembling an unsteady flame, splendorous as young lightning, makes three and a half coils around the void.

Now mentally repeat the seed mantra LANG (phonetically pronounced "luhng") at least ten times as you imagine LANG, of yellow color, is vibrating within the chakra itself . . . [Record fifteen seconds of silence here.]

Then move your attention up to the "sacral chakra," the seat of procreation, located in the spine's pelvic area. Imagine a lotus flower with six vermilion petals, radiating both red and golden energies that circulate throughout your blood and lymph systems. In the chakra's center is a pure white crescent moon, which embodies the water element. Responsible for bodily circulation and muscular movements, this chakra brings health and vitality to all your organs.

Now mentally repeat the seed mantra VANG (phonetically pronounced "vuhng") at least ten times as you imagine VANG, of pure white color, vibrating within the chakra itself . . . [Record fifteen seconds of silence here.]

Next place attention on your "navel chakra," the center of willpower and regulator of digestion, located in your spine on the same horizontal plane as your navel. Envision a beautiful, radiant ten-petalled lotus of black color, shining like millions of suns. Within the lotus, a brilliant red triangle points downwards, embodying the fire element.

The petals radiate life force energy, known as *prana* in India, *chi* in China, and *ki* in Japan. Because the navel chakra holds the greatest concentration of intense life energy, prana circulates from there throughout your subtle body.

Now mentally repeat the seed mantra RANG (phonetically pronounced "ruhng") at least ten times as you imagine RANG, of black color, vibrating within the chakra itself . . . [Record fifteen seconds of silence here.]

Next place attention on a point in your spine on the same horizontal plane as the point between your nipples in your chest. This is known as "heart chakra," the seat of consciousness and gateway to the infinite. It regulates your heart, lungs, and thymus.

Envision a fragrant lotus with twelve petals radiating and shining deep red. In its center, a six-pointed star embodies the air element. The upward-pointing triangle represents higher awareness and returning to the divine source. The downward-pointing triangle signifies earthly material pursuits and entanglement in illusion. At the balance point between the upper and lower regions, this chakra is the gateway to both spiritual and material worlds.

Within the six-pointed star, a red triangle points downwards, shining with the brilliance of ten million lightning flashes. The triangle represents internal focus rather than external sensory stimuli. Within the triangle is a nameless, formless, quality-less void—the concentrated singularity of pure consciousness. Seated in the triangle, a still eternal flame, tapering upward, burns in a windless place. It is the spark of your soul—golden, resplendent, luminous, and motionless.

Now mentally repeat the seed mantra YANG (phonetically pronounced "yuhng") at least ten times as you imagine YANG, of smoky gray color, is vibrating within the chakra . . . [Record fifteen seconds of silence here.]

Next place attention in the cervical area at the back of your neck, associated with the cervical plexus and thyroid gland. This "throat chakra," which embodies the ether element, regulates creative expression and invention. Imagine a sixteen-petalled lotus of shining smoke color. In its center, a pure white void circular region blazes like the full moon. A smoke-colored triangle resides in the center of the void, and the lotus filaments are red.

Now mentally repeat the seed mantra HANG (phonetically pronounced "huhng") at least ten times as you imagine HANG, of snow-white color, is vibrating within the chakra . . . [Record fifteen seconds of silence here.]

Now place attention in the center of your skull, where your "third eye chakra" is seated at the pineal gland. See a lotus with two petals vibrating with nectarous cool rays and intense lightning-white color. One petal radiates pure power of white color downward through the five lower chakras. The other petal radiates towards the upper chakras. Imagine these two radiations merging into one, which brings your awareness into oneness and wholeness.

This chakra, called the "command center," distributes life energy throughout the body. A portal between the physical and subtler realms, this eye of higher consciousness is the seat of your mind and higher self, and center of illumination, intuition, super-sensory perception, wisdom, and spiritual discernment. It regulates the pineal gland, cavernous plexus, and biological rhythms.

In the chakra's blazing red hexagonal region, the nectar of immortality abides. There a white point of radiating masculine energy is seated within a triangle of feminine energy. The triangle embodies the primordial seed mantra OM, which gives rise to the entire universe. Kundalini, a luminous circle of light, rests in this chakra as splendorous, pure, aroused consciousness.

Now mentally repeat the seed mantra OM (phonetically pronounced "ohm") at least ten times as you imagine OM, of blazing moon-white color, is vibrating within the chakra . . . [Record fifteen seconds of silence here.]

Then visualize the "crown chakra" lotus of one thousand petals like an umbrella just above your head. Its petals shine white like the moon. Its lightning-like splendorous filaments are red. Its petals, the abode of all powers and vibrations, emit both light and sound in a thousand light beams.

Envision a circular full moon region at the chakra's center—shining golden with countless light rays. Seated in a brilliant triangle is an infinitely concentrated circular void, a point of unlimited potential and energy. Nectarous and delightful, it is the home of supreme

Spirit, the abode of immortality. There, masculine and feminine energies merge in perfect union. In that point of oneness, the source of supreme bliss, awareness becomes superconsciousness, and liberation is bestowed.

Now. spend a few minutes in that concentrated point of perfect, absolute bliss . . . [Record three minutes of silence here.]

Then, with gratitude in your heart, keep your eyes closed as you come forth from the meditation by taking at least four deep vigorous breaths and pretend you are blowing out four candles . . . [Record fifteen seconds of silence here.] If you feel the need to blow out more candles, please do so before opening your eyes . . . Then, come all the way back to objective and subjective balance and open your eyes . . .

Now repeat the following affirmation audibly with your eyes open:

I AM alert . . . I AM awake . . . I AM very alert . . . I AM very awake . . . I AM objectively and subjectively balanced . . . I AM in control . . . I AM the only authority in my life . . . I AM divinely protected by the light of my being . . . Thank you, Spirit, and SO IT IS.

After practicing the meditations and affirmations in this chapter, please describe in your journal what you experienced. In the next chapter, you'll open the doorway to ascension and physical immortality.

Chapter 18

Open the Doorway to Ascension

"Ascension" is the attainment of physical immortality, and an "ascended master" has transformed the human physical body into a light body, which can appear to anyone, anywhere, at any time, in any form. Ascended masters have command over all the laws of nature and elements of nature. They are guardians of the planet and assist in human evolution.

GREAT DEATH-CONQUERING MANTRA

The "Maha Mrityunjaya Mantra," also know as "Tryambakam Mantra," is chanted by millions of Hindus throughout the world. It's a divine armor that can protect you from harm, illness, and untimely death.

Please learn how to pronounce the mantra before trying to recite it. Simply search the Rajshri Soul YouTube channel for "Mrityunjaya Mantra 108 Times Chanting."

Please say this mantra audibly in a clear voice, with conviction:

OM Tryambakam Yajaamahay.
Sugandhim Pushti Vardhanam.
Uravaarukam Iva Bandhanaan.
Mrityor Muksheeya Maamritaat.

Here's a translation of the mantra:

*"OM. I worship and adore you, O three-eyed one, O Shiva. You
are sweet gladness, the fragrance of life. You nourish me, restore
my health, and cause me to thrive. As, in due time, the stem of
the cucumber weakens and falls from the vine, so liberate me from
bondage, attachment, and death, and do not withhold immortality."*

ASCENSION VISUALIZATION

The glorious state of ascension is attained by transforming the physical
body into a light body. Your corporeal body is made of five elements.
In this ascension visualization, you'll imagine systematically breaking
down these bodily elements into their primal components. Then you'll
arrive at the most fundamental constituents of creation—light and
sound: *"In the beginning was the Word, and the Word was with God, and the
Word was God."*[1] The most fundamental Word is OM—the primordial
hum of creation, from which the entire universe springs. Primal sound

is the progenitor of primal light: *"And God said, 'Let there be light: and there was light.'"*[2] With that statement, the Creator speaks light into being.

I received this special, unique visualization directly from the ascended master Babaji, the immortal saint of Badrinath, Himalayas, said to be 5000 years old. You can read about him in my book, *Ascension: Connecting with the Immortal Masters and Beings of Light*.

Please record this visualization onto your device:

Now get comfortable in your chair. If you are listening to this as a recording, please close your eyes and keep them closed until I tell you to open them.

Now just relax. Take a big deep breath. Breathe in . . . and out . . . Take a deep breath to get settled and relaxed. Breathe in . . . and out . . . Take a deep breath to go deeper. Breathe in . . . and out . . . Then relax and breathe normally.

We now call forth the great immortal sage Babaji to lead this beautiful visualization, to bring forth as much of the ascension experience as you can possibly comfortably enjoy at this time. Take a deep breath and go deeper. Breathe in . . . and let it go . . . Take another big deep breath to relax. Breathe in . . . and let go . . . Now breathe normally.

In this visualization, you will imagine disassembling your physical body layer by layer. You will envision the elementary components of bodily matter being absorbed, and the gross material body being transmuted into finer and finer material. You will break down and consume the body's fundamental components, reducing its constituents to nothingness.

You will picture the five elements being dissolved one by one, until your entire physical body is subsumed by light and becomes a light body. However, do not fear. This is only a visualization. After it is over, you will be intact and still have a physical body. You will not disappear, and your body will not dissolve.

Take a big deep breath of relaxation. Breathe in . . . and relax . . . Take another deep breath and go even deeper. Breathe in . . . and let go. Now breathe normally. Deeper, deeper, deeper, into the wells of Spirit, into the silence of being. Let go and be at peace. Now become aware of the body, which is comfortable and deeply relaxed. Become aware of the mind, which is quiet, still, and at peace. Now take a big deep breath and go deeper. Breathe in . . . and out . . . Now breathe normally. You are comfortable, relaxed, and at rest.

Your physical body is composed of material matter, made of the five elements: earth, water, fire, air, and space, also known as ether. Earth is the grossest bodily element, and space is the subtlest. Between the atoms of your body, there is empty space. Your body is composed of one millionth of one percent atoms and the rest empty space. Therefore, your body is almost entirely composed of space.

Now take a deep breath. Breathe in . . . and let it go . . . Then breathe normally. You are divinely protected and completely safe during this process. When you come out of this visualization, you will still be here. So just relax into it, and follow my voice.

Breathe in . . . and out . . . Then breathe normally. Let go, let go, let go, let go. Let go, let go, let God. Peace, peace, be still. Be still and be at peace. Take a big deep breath to go deeper. Breathe in . . . and out . . . Then breathe normally.

The physical body is made of the earth element. Notice the matter in your physical body, which is made of this gross substance of earth. But you will imagine this material body dissolving and getting reduced into its primary elements, layer by layer. Take a big deep breath. Breathe in . . . and out . . . Release, release, release. Release and be at peace. Completely let go, completely give up, completely relax.

Now envision the gross physical matter of the earth element in your body now starting to melt and dissolve. It is becoming liquid, like water. It is beginning to dissolve and becoming very malleable, very flexible, very much like water. Very fluid. The body is becoming fluid, like water. Your physical body is becoming like water. It is being lique-fied. From the top of the head, the body is starting to melt and dissolve into liquid. Shoulders, chest, hips, legs, feet. The body is melting and liquefying, like water.

Breathe in . . . and out . . . Then breathe normally. Peace, peace, be still. Be still and be at peace. Do not be afraid. Just practice the visualization. You will be fine. You will still have a body afterwards. There is nothing to fear. Just let go and allow.

Now visualize your body melting and becoming fluid. It is flowing like liquid. Your body is becoming like a liquid—flowing and fluid, without edges or borders. The physical matter of your body is no longer solid and hard. It no longer has boundaries. It is melting into liquid. It is liquefying. It is starting to flow like water. The earth element is being absorbed by the water element.

Now take a deep breath and go deeper. Breathe in . . . and let it go . . . Then breathe normally. Imagine the body now breaking down into its subtler elements, step by step. It is now becoming like fire. That liquefied body is now being heated up in fire. That water is beginning to boil, and the body is turning into steam. The body is evaporating into steam. Now envision the body dissolving in the fire. The body is starting to be consumed by fire. The water element is now being absorbed by the fire element.

Now take another big deep breath. Breathe in . . . and out . . . Then breathe normally. Do not be afraid. All is well. You will return to your normal physical form after you come out. Just relax and continue to practice the visualization.

Now imagine the body is ignited, burning, and steaming. It is being entirely consumed by fire. That fire is aflame, blazing, and smoldering. The entire body is now getting cremated and burnt to ashes. The body is becoming like ash. It is being entirely consumed until it turns to ash. Just picture the body becoming a pile of ash.

Now take a deep breath and go deeper. Breathe in . . . and out . . . Then breathe normally. The body is now being reduced into its subtler and subtler elements, step by step, layer by layer.

Now visualize the air element. The wind comes to blow the ash away, blowing the ash away. Blowing, blowing, blowing away the ash. That ash is now blown away by the wind. Your entire body is now becoming like air—very light and filled with air. Your body is now permeated by air. There is nothing left of your body but air. The wind is surging throughout your body, which is now transparent, like air. The fire element is now entirely consumed by the air element.

Now take a deep breath and go deeper. Breathe in . . . and let it go . . . Then breathe normally. Your body is no longer solid. No longer fire, no longer ash, no longer water, no longer earth. It has become air. The body is now lighter than earth, lighter than water, lighter than fire. Your body is suffused with air and is weightless. Your body is filled with the air element. It is perfectly light and made entirely of air.

Now take a deep breath and go deeper. Breathe in . . . and let it go . . . Then breathe normally. You are safe and protected. No harm will come to your body. It will be intact when you return from this visualization.

Now imagine your body is becoming like space. Your body is becoming empty space. Your body now floats in a vacuum, free from gravity, without any resistance. Your body is now the element of space, lighter than air, lighter than anything. Nothing is left of your body but empty space.

Your body is lighter and lighter, lighter and lighter, lighter and lighter than air, and lifting and lifting and lifting and lifting, and lighter than air. Your body has become space. Because your body is nothing but space, it is empty and void. Your body is so light that it no longer has any substance to it. The element of space has consumed the air element. Your body has dissolved entirely into space.

Take a deep breath. Breathe in . . . and out . . . Then breathe normally. Do not be afraid. All is well. You will not dissolve. You will not disappear. Your body will still be here after this meditation. Just follow this visualization.

Now picture your body as pure space. Where there was a body, there is now space, completely free from all boundaries and limitations. Because it is made of space, and space is everywhere, your body is now everywhere, boundless and unlimited. Your body dissolves into the emptiness of space. It has become all worlds and all beings. It has become the universe.

Take a deep breath. Breathe in . . . and out . . . Then breathe normally. Now envision the element of space is being consumed by light. The space element is now being saturated with pure light. Your body is dissolving into light. Divine light is filling your body now. You are becoming a light being. You are now bathed in pure light, of whatever color you see, whether clear, white, golden, or all colors of the rainbow.

Rays of pure divine light are filling your entire body now, which is transparent, lighter than space, glowing with illumination, shining with radiance, and gleaming with beauteous brilliance. Your body is now filled with dazzling luminescence—resplendent and blazing with light. Beams of divine light fill your body and radiate and vibrate from within you to surround your body. Your body is now consumed by divine light and made entirely of light. There is nothing left of your body but pure light. Your body is transformed into light. You are light.

Take a deep breath now. Breathe in . . . and out . . . Then breathe normally. Allow that light to vibrate, to radiate, to fill you, to surround you, to lift you. You are now a being of light. You are now pure light. You are everywhere present in the light.

Now enjoy this divine light for a few moments in silence. Breathe in . . . and out . . . Allow that light to vibrate and radiate within and around you. You are that light, the light of Spirit . . . [Record one minute of silence.]

Now repeat the following affirmation audibly in a clear and confident voice:

The light of Spirit fills and surrounds me now . . . I AM filled with the radiance of Spirit . . . I AM the light of Spirit . . . I AM the light body . . . I AM filled with pure light . . . I AM an immortal being of light . . . I AM the resurrection and the life . . . I AM the ascension now . . . I AM an ascended master now . . . I AM perfection everywhere now . . . I AM perfection here now . . . Thank you, Spirit, and SO IT IS . . .

Now, with deep gratitude in your heart, you will come forth from the visualization, integrating this exquisite, pure light of ascension into your everyday life. If you are listening to a recording, please keep your eyes closed until I tell you to open them.

Now lean forward slightly and pretend to vigorously blow out a candle . . . Coming forth from the level of Spirit, now bring forth this divine light of ascension into your subconscious mind. Now vigorously blow out another candle . . . Come forth now, knowing this divine light is integrated into your conscious mind, and your mind is transforming into divine mind and divine light. Now vigorously blow out another candle . . . Come forth now, knowing this beautiful light is now integrated into your physical form, feeling lightness, vital robust health, and well-being in the body.

Now blow out another candle . . . knowing this divine light is now integrated into your everyday life and your environment. You have been permanently transformed, lifted, awakened, and lightened by this meditation. This divine light continues with you, throughout this day and every day. This beautiful ascension experience is now integrated into your life, and you are experiencing your physical form as lighter from now on.

Now, keeping your eyes closed, become aware of your body and your feet flat on the floor, very grounded, very alert, very awake, very present, feeling wonderful. Now blow out another candle . . . knowing that as you come forth from this meditation, you see yourself as a divine being of radiant light. You are filled with the light of Spirit.

Now, keeping your eyes closed, vigorously blow out four more candles . . . [Record fifteen seconds of silence here.] Then come all the way back to inward and outward balance and open your eyes. If you do not feel like opening your eyes, go ahead and blow out more candles first, and then open your eyes . . . If needed, blow out more candles, and then eyes wide open . . .

Now repeat the following affirmation audibly with your eyes open:

I AM alert . . . I AM very alert . . . I AM awake . . . I AM very awake . . . I AM inwardly and outwardly balanced . . . I AM in control . . . I AM the only authority in my life . . . I AM divinely protected by the light of my being . . . Thank you, God, and SO IT IS.

Now take a few moments to write in your journal and describe what you experienced by practicing the visualization and mantra in this chapter. More information about how you can take your meditation practice to the next level is next—in the Epilogue.

Epilogue

Now that you've partaken of various meditative appetizers by practicing the methods in this book, you can move on to the main course and take your meditation practice to the next level. The best way to develop your ability to experience deep meditation and to cultivate your intuitive abilities is to practice, practice, practice. Make meditation a daily routine, and keep practicing it regularly.

Most importantly, don't be afraid to make mistakes. On your path to higher consciousness, you might make mistakes—especially when receiving intuition and following inner guidance. But don't let that deter you from continuing your practice. Just like any skill in life, such as playing the piano, you can't learn without making mistakes. At first you'll make errors. But with practice, you can get better. If you stick with it, you can master it. So it is with meditation. Keep doing it regularly and you can succeed.

In this book you've learned some powerful methods, such as guided meditation, affirmation, and mantras. However, you might feel a desire to study more. With that in mind, I recommend my book *Exploring Meditation* to learn about:

1. Meditation logistics: how, where, when, what, and why.

2. How to deal with difficulties you might encounter while meditating.

3. What to do about uncomfortable experiences during or after meditation.

4. How to deal with unusual experiences cropping up during meditation.

5. What to do when meditation fails.

6. An extensive overview of Eastern wisdom.

Practicing the methods in this book has set you on a path to developing your intuition and communicating with your higher self. But if you want to go deeper, I recommend you study my book *Awaken Your Divine Intuition*. That book can help you:

1. Experience direct contact with Spirit.

2. Open to your higher self and receive intuitive guidance clearly.

3. Test whether your intuition is real using my field-proven ten-test system.

4. Learn how to heal blockages during meditative and intuitive
   practices.

In this book you've been introduced to chakras and your energy field. You can learn more in my books *Awaken Your Third Eye, The Power of Auras, The Big Book of Chakras and Chakra Healing,* and *Color Your Chakras.* In this book you've practiced many affirmations. In my book *Instant Healing,* there are 243 affirmations you can use for healing and transformation. Using the methods in this book, you've called upon ascended masters and beings of light. You can read stories about these divine beings in my fascinating book *Ascension.* And to learn more about what really happens on the spiritual path, you can read my memoir: *Maharishi & Me: Seeking Enlightenment with the Beatles' Guru.*

Your life is a treasure, so make the most of every precious moment. Spirit is continually knocking, waiting for you to open the door. Open it and allow the flood of ecstasy to pour into your being. Happy meditating and enjoy the bliss!

Acknowledgments

I am grateful to those who have helped bring this book to press. I have the greatest gratitude, respect, and admiration for Jeff and Deborah Herman, who have been amazing advisors and loyal friends for twenty-five years. I thank Michael Pye and Laurie Kelly-Pye, who have stood by me for nearly two decades. Thank you to Kasandra Cook, Jane Hagaman, and everyone else at Weiser Books, who have worked diligently to bring this book to publication.

I give special thanks to my mentors, including Maharishi Mahesh Yogi, Peter Victor Meyer, Raman Kumar Bachchan, and all my inner teachers and divine beings of light, including the immortal Babaji and Holy Spirit. Without the influence of these saintly teachers, I would have no experience of meditation and no comprehension of subtle energies.

Appendix

Choose Your Meditation

Endnotes

Chapter 1

1. *www.sacred-texts.com/bud/sbe10/sbe1003.htm*.

2. Holy Bible, Matthew 15:11: *www.biblegateway.com*.

Chapter 2

1. https://nccih.nih.gov/health/meditation/overview.htm.

Chapter 18

1. Holy Bible, John 1:1: *www.biblegateway.com*.

2. Holy Bible, Genesis 1:3: *www.biblegateway.com*.

Other Books by the Author

Divine Revelation. New York: Fireside / Touchstone / Simon & Schuster, 1996.

Exploring Meditation. Newburyport, MA: Red Wheel / Weiser / New Page, 2002.

Miracle Prayer. Berkeley, CA: Celestial Arts / Penguin Random House, 2006.

Ascension. Newburyport, MA: Red Wheel / Weiser / New Page, 2010.

Instant Healing. Newburyport, MA: Red Wheel / Weiser / New Page, 2013.

The Power of Auras. Newburyport, MA: Red Wheel / Weiser / New Page, 2013.

The Power of Chakras. Newburyport, MA: Red Wheel / Weiser / New Page, 2013.

Awaken Your Divine Intuition. Newburyport, MA: Red Wheel / Weiser / New Page, 2016.

Awaken Your Third Eye. Newburyport, MA: Red Wheel / Weiser / New Page, 2016.

Color Your Chakras. Newburyport, MA: Red Wheel / Weiser / New Page, 2016.

Maharishi & Me. New York: Skyhorse Publishing, 2018.

The Big Book of Chakras and Chakra Healing. Newburyport, MA: Red Wheel / Weiser / New Page, 2019.

Earth Energy Meditations. Newburyport, MA: Weiser, 2020.

About the Author

Dr. Susan Shumsky has dedicated her life to helping people take command of their lives in highly effective, powerful, positive ways. She is a leading spirituality expert, highly acclaimed and greatly respected professional speaker, sought-after media guest, New Thought minister, and Doctor of Divinity.

Dr. Shumsky has won thirty-one book awards and is the author of seventeen books in English and thirty-four books in other languages, including *Divine Revelation*, published by Simon & Schuster; *Miracle Prayer*, published by Penguin Random House; *Exploring Meditation, Ascension, Instant Healing, The Power of Auras, Awaken Your Third Eye, Awaken Your Divine Intuition, Color Your Chakras, The Big Book of Chakras, Third Eye Meditations*, and *Earth Energy Meditations*, published by Red Wheel/Weiser. Her memoir *Maharishi & Me*, published by Skyhorse Publishing, has won twelve book awards. Several books were #1 *amazon.com* bestsellers, and two were One Spirit Book Club selections.

Dr. Shumsky has practiced self-development disciplines since 1967. For over two decades she practiced deep meditation for many hours daily in the Himalayas, the Swiss Alps, and other secluded areas under the personal guidance of the enlightened master from India, Maharishi Mahesh Yogi, founder of Transcendental Meditation and guru of the Beatles, Deepak Chopra, and other major celebrities. Dr. Shumsky served on Maharishi's personal staff for six of those years in Spain, Mallorca, Austria, Italy, and Switzerland.

Dr. Shumsky was not born with any supernormal faculties but developed her expertise through decades of patient daily study and practice. She has taught yoga, meditation, prayer, and intuition to thousands of students worldwide since 1970 as a pioneer in the consciousness field. She is founder of Divine Revelation®, a unique, field-proven technology for contacting the divine presence, hearing and testing the inner voice, and receiving clear divine guidance.

Dr. Shumsky travels extensively, producing and facilitating workshops, conferences, ocean cruise seminars, and tours to sacred destinations worldwide. She also offers teleseminars and private spiritual coaching, prayer therapy sessions, and spiritual breakthrough sessions.

All of Dr. Shumsky's years of research into consciousness and inner exploration have contributed to her books and teachings, which can significantly reduce many pitfalls in a seeker's quest for inner truth and greatly shorten the time required for the inner pathway to Spirit.

On her websites, *www.drsusan.org* and *www.divinetravels.com*, you can:

- Join the mailing list.

- See Dr. Shumsky's itinerary.

- Read Chapter 1 of Dr. Shumsky's books.

- Listen to free interviews, read articles, and watch videos of Dr. Shumsky.

- Find Divine Revelation teachers in various areas.

- Order books, audio and video products, downloadable files, home study courses, and laminated cards of healing affirmations.

- Order beautiful, full-color prints of Dr. Shumsky's illustrations.

- Register for telephone sessions and teleseminars with Dr. Shumsky.

- Register for one of her spiritual cruises, retreats, or tours.

When you join the mailing list at *www.drsusan.org*, you will receive a free, downloadable, guided mini-meditation plus access to our free online community group forum and free weekly teleconference prayer circle.

As a gift for reading this book, please use the following special discount code when you register for one of the spiritual cruises, retreats, or tours at *www.divinetravels.com*: MEDITATION108.

We want to hear from you. Please write about your personal experiences of meditation or invite Dr. Shumsky to speak to your group: divinerev@aol.com. If you enjoyed this book, please write a customer review on Amazon.com, and please give the book to friends and family as gifts.

To Our Readers

Weiser Books, an imprint of Red Wheel/Weiser, publishes books across the entire spectrum of occult, esoteric, speculative, and New Age subjects. Our mission is to publish quality books that will make a difference in people's lives without advocating any one particular path or field of study. We value the integrity, originality, and depth of knowledge of our authors.

Our readers are our most important resource, and we appreciate your input, suggestions, and ideas about what you would like to see published.

Visit our website at *www.redwheelweiser.com* to learn about our upcoming books and free downloads, and be sure to go to *www.redwheelweiser.com/newsletter* to sign up for newsletters and exclusive offers.

You can also contact us at *info@rwwbooks.com* or at

Red Wheel/Weiser, LLC
65 Parker Street, Suite 7
Newburyport, MA 01950